Each stitch that we take is a step in the sewing journey and every traveler creates her own map of the world.

Introduction

Stitch Journeys is a call to be adventurous and an invitation to explore. Using the many specialty threads from WonderFil™ and perhaps some new-to-you techniques, we hope that these journeys will spark your wanderlust and sense of curiosity in sewing. Far from difficult or intimidating, the techniques and projects within are offered to inspire and broaden your creative landscape.

Why specifically focus on thread as a creative tool? Unlike strongly patterned fabrics, thread is a non-determined medium. It has infinite potential to become anything that you want it to become. You, as the artist (stitcher, sewist, quilter, or creator) direct the flow of color, line and texture. You make your own rules and develop your own style.

Throughout this book you will find the pages of a stitch sketchbook. These samples of threads and techniques are presented in an easy to recreate 4x6 format that we are calling your *passport pages*. Some of these techniques re-appear in projects or gallery pieces, while others are simply there for your reference and inspiration.

Instructions are offered as guideposts to help you get started. Should you need more in-depth directions, a selected reading list is provided to help take your project forward.

Meeting the inhabitants of the places you visit enriches traveling. Such is the case with our guest artists. They will share with you their art as well as their own tips and techniques for exploring with WonderFil threads.

We encourage you to try all of the techniques and to sample WonderFil's many specialty threads. The variety of weights and textures that they offer are like no others. We believe that they will open up worlds of stitching discoveries for you.

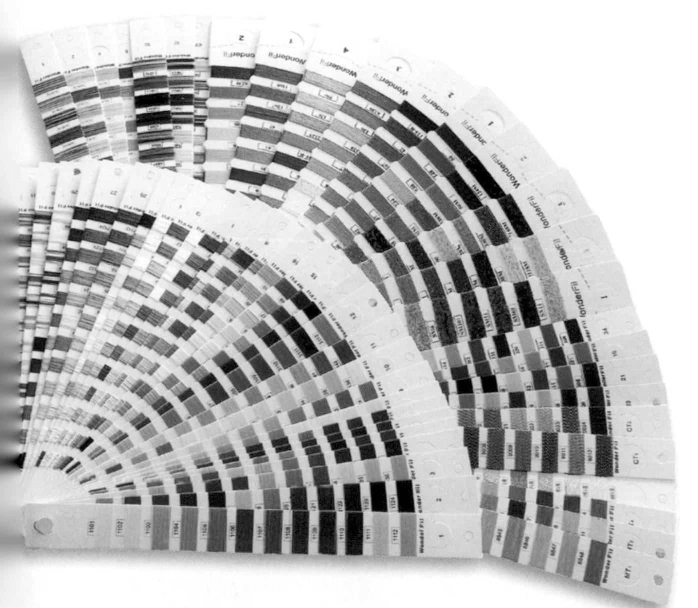

Bon voyage,

Deb and Liz

A Journey of a thousand miles begins with a single step.
~ Lao-Tzu

The Threads

WonderFil has taken thread from the role of an under-appreciated and often invisible tool of sewing and made it into a specialized instrument for your creating. Gone are the days of the "one size fits all needs" sewing thread. As a sewist, you know that threads serve many different roles in your stitching and creating. Be it for piecing, quilting, embellishing or creating structure, threads serve different purposes. Sometimes their presence is obvious and showy, while other times you need them to disappear into your work. It might help to think of threads as theatrical players. Sometimes they are in a supporting role. At other times they will be co-stars, stars or even blockbuster mega-stars! The casting is up to you. Getting to know your thread will open up new possibilities for your work. By understanding how they blend or stand out, or how they add texture to your work, you will begin to use them in new and varied ways.

The following is an overview of each type of WonderFil thread and its suggested uses. Once you begin working with them, we are sure that you will discover even more uses for each one.

InvisaFil is extremely delicate yet also an incredibly strong 100wt soft polyester thread. It is a great choice for sewing on delicate fabrics such as sheers, organdy and silk. When quilting, it's perfect to use in any application where you want the fabric or texture to star. InvisaFil is especially suitable for invisible appliqué, quilting in the ditch, fine stippling, trapunto and use for couching on beads, trims and heavy threads. Use InvisaFil in the bobbin for intricate appliqué work, especially on delicate fabrics.

DecoBob is slightly heavier than InvisaFil and yet still retains the soft hand that InvisaFil offers. An 80wt all purpose polyester thread, it will become the workhorse of your studio. Use DecoBob for the same applications as InvisaFil where extra strength is required such as embroidered clothing, buttonholes and bed quilts. DecoBob is also great for piecing quilts, as it adds no bulk to seams, and for use with home decorating fabrics.

Silco is a wonderfully versatile thread. It's 40wt cotton and 100% lint free. You will rarely need to clean out the bobbin case. Silco is available in 30 solid colors and 30 variegated colors making it perfect for quilting, embellishment, embroidery, and general sewing for those that prefer a cotton thread or a matte finish.

The *Rayon* collection is amazing in its variety of solid and variegated colors. At 40wt with a silky finish and wonderfully vibrant colors, they are great for machine and hand embroidery, embellishment, thread painting and appliqué. With 342 solid colors and 31 variegated colors, you will always be able to find the perfect shade for your project.

Mirage is another rayon collection. It's 30wt and random space dyed in an incredible selection of colors. Slightly heavier than regular rayon and easy to use, it is wonderful for embellishment, hand and machine embroidery, thread paint and appliqué. The 40 variegated colors are so spectacular that you will want to own them all.

D-Twist is made up of two 40wt rayon threads twisted together in coordinating colors. The extra twist gives a wonderful effect of dimension and texture. D-Twist is great in embroidery, embellishment and as thread paint.

Accent is like no other thread available. It's a 12 wt, two-ply rayon that can be used through a size 14 or 16 topstitch needle in your machine. Its large size gives dimension and depth to your project and can quickly fill in background areas of embroidery. It can be used in embellishment, hand and machine embroidery, thread painting and appliqué.

Razzle and Dazzle Rayon are comparable to a size eight crochet thread. They have an incredible silky feel with rich colors and a high sheen. They can be used in the bobbin for machine sewing, hand embroidery, couching, crochet, knitting, tassels and fringes. Dazzle has a metallic thread woven in for an extra sparkle in your work.

The *Metallic* collection is rayon-based to give a smooth, soft touch and added strength to prevent breaking even when sewing at high speeds. The Metallic threads work well in embellishment, hand and machine embroidery, and thread paint.

Hologram is a fun thread that is highly reflective for extra shimmer and brilliance. Use it in embellishment, hand and machine embroidery projects, and thread painting.

Sizzle is a four-ply metallic thread that is used like Razzle and Dazzle for bobbin work, hand embroidery, couching, crochet, knitting, tassels and fringes. It will add an incredible sparkle and texture to your projects.

Packing For Your Journey

- Threads
- Needles
- Fabric and embellishment bits and pieces
- Extra bobbins
- Extra bobbin case
- Thread stand
- Hoops
- Wonderguards

Seasoned "travelers" develop a packing list of items that they count on having for their travels, things that make travel easier. Here are some "must-have" and "nice to have" supplies that will make your journey more rewarding.

Threads: We have traditionally been taught to have the basic black, white, gray and a neutral blender on hand and this is still important. However, with WonderFil's lush palette of colors at your disposal, you can expand beyond the basics to a world full of possibility. One can simply never have too much thread.

Needles: No one needle suits every purpose, particularly when working with specialty threads. Needles vary in thickness, size of eye, shape and sharpness of point. Generally, finer fabrics and threads can use smaller needle sizes (lower numbers indicate a finer needle while higher numbers indicate a sturdier needle). Heavier threads require a heavier needle to punch a larger hole but also need a larger eye to accommodate the thread (such as that in a topstitch needle). Metallic threads work best with less friction. A metallic needle tapers to have less contact with the thread and has a large eye to allow the thread to flow freely. Embroidery needles are shaped for high-speed stitching. Specialty needles such as twin or hemstitch allow for specialty stitching and are great to have on hand in a variety of sizes. The most commonly used needle for the projects in this book is a size 14 embroidery needle. It is excellent for free motion sewing, surface embroidery and many of the techniques you will want to try for yourself. Keep a good stock of needles on hand. This will keep you sewing till 3a.m.!

TIP: Change your needle after every project or if you sense a change in the sound or feel of your sewing or if you have difficulties with your thread fraying and breaking.

Fabric and embellishment bits and pieces: Many of the projects herein require small amounts of fabrics. Often a simple fat quarter of any one fabric will do. It's the bits and pieces of specialty fabrics such as silks, laces and organzas that will add just the right touch. Collect these bits as you find them and you will build a stash that will serve you well:

- batik and blender fabrics that will let your threadwork shine
- "specials" such as lace, velvet, silk or organza
- felt
- assortment of beads
- Angelina® Fibers
- assorted yarns and ribbons

Hoops: Often used with free motion sewing and for extra stability, machine embroidery hoops come in a variety of sizes. Look for a hoop that is both thin enough to fit easily under the needle and strong enough to hold the fabric tight. Some inexpensive hoops loosen easily and allow the fabric to relax too much. Be sure to get a hoop that isn't too large for your machine, remembering that the radius can't be any larger than the distance between your needle and the inside of your machine bed. We specifically have found German embroidery hoops to be excellent.

Bobbins: Don't be afraid of having lots of extra bobbins available. There is nothing more frustrating than having to unspool an entire bobbin because it isn't the right thread for your project. Use bobbin boxes to organize your collections of different thread weights.

Bobbin Case: The investment in an extra bobbin case for use with heavy threads is well worth it. Some sewing machine manufacturers make extra cases specifically designed for use with heavy threads. Clean your bobbin case and housing often. Each time you need to rewind your bobbin, take 10 seconds to de-lint and/or oil your bobbin housing as recommended by your machine manufacturer.

Stabilizers: An important hidden helper in your stitching, stabilizers keep fabric laying flat. They give thread and its associated tension something more than the fabric to "bite" into. Stabilizers also keep fabric from tearing with heavy stitching. They improve the appearance of machine embroidery and threadwork. Stabilizers are available as woven or non-woven, stitch-in, fusible, heat reactive or water-soluble and they come in light, medium and heavy weights. Your local sewing store can help you choose the one you need but don't be afraid to experiment. You will develop your own favorites and will want to have a variety on hand.

Thread Stand: A separate thread stand allows for accommodating larger spools and gives specialty threads extra space to unspool without twisting and kinking. Some threads need some distance between the spool and the needle. If you don't have a thread stand try standing your thread spool in a cup or jar beside of your machine.

Wonderguard Wraps: These self-cling wraps not only keep threads tidy and dust free, they also can be used during sewing to keep threads from improperly unwinding off the spool while you work.

Sewing Machine: The techniques used in this book do not require a fancy or expensive machine. Magic can be made with simple straight and zigzag stitches. The ability to lower the feed dogs makes free motion sewing easier.

The Passport

A passport officially sanctions travel abroad. It gives permission to be an adventurer and the visas within document your journey. Your stitched passport similarly documents your stitch travels. In it, you can record all of your stitching adventures and maybe even a few detours and daring misadventures. Who knows where you will go?

Why create a passport? The intrepid traveler immerses herself in the language and customs of the country she visits. After all, the best way to learn is by doing! The small size of the passport page allows for fearless experimentation and play without the pressure of wasting time and materials. We chose 4x6 but you can choose any size you are comfortable with, 5x7, 6x6, 8x8. We don't recommend that you go larger than 8x8 because then it becomes a project and not play.

The beauty of your passport is that you can always add to it. Whenever you want to try a new technique, you can document your adventure with a new page. You can also have fun with "filler pages": rubber-stamped, painted or otherwise playfully embellished pages that are made just for fun.

TEMPLATE

It is very easy to create a page:

1. Make a template of your page out of template plastic (available in quilt shops). Make it the size of your finished pages. Mark it with placement holes so that you can consistently mark binding holes on each page.
2. Cut fabric, batting and stabilizer (as needed) to slightly larger than finished size.
3. Be sure to work within your page size and leave room to one side for binding holes.
4. Try out your technique. Experiment. Play. Test your boundaries.
5. Once your page is complete, trim it to your template size. Use the holes in the template to mark holes for eyelets or buttonholes.
6. Stitch two finished pages wrong sides together to form a complete page. Finish the edges as desired (zigzag, decorative stitch, couched thread or fiber, wrapped with binding or trim, etc.).
7. Line up the binding holes on each side and either set eyelets or stitch buttonholes.
8. Finished pages are joined by two binder rings (from office supply or hardware store). These rings can be embellished as desired.

When suggesting that you try a technique in passport format, we note it with P.S.
P.S. = passport suggestion (suggested passport page subject)

P.S. Get started by creating a few pages with stitch outs of the different threads like we did. Make a template shape (heart, square, or rectangle). Mark it out on a fabric that is backed with fusible web. Fill in your shape with stitches: straight, patterned and stipple stitch. Cut out your shape and fuse it to a blank passport page. Voilà! You have started on your adventure!

COLOR WORK & TENSION PLAY

Volumes have been written about color in design. Color is often the first element that the viewer reacts to. Color comes not only from fabric but also from thread and surface embellishment. Thread color can be used to subtly reflect a fabric or pattern's colors or it can strongly contrast with them. Thread color can blend into fabric and provide texture and shadow. It can tone down or enliven a fabric choice. It can also be used to artfully shade a thread painting.

Use a color wheel to help you to make thread choices. By simply reading the instructions that come with most wheels, you can gain knowledge of basic color theory. Soon you will be able to skillfully work with warm and cool colors. Analogous and complementary color schemes will make more sense and color value will be seen in the subtle variations of the WonderFil thread palette.

We say "color work" because the use of color is worth working at. There is a science to color theory. Use this theory to better understand your color preferences. Experimenting with color in your passport pages gives you a simple, small format to work in.

P.S.
- **Try making your own color wheel of thread.**
- **Experiment with color theory. Try an analogous or a complementary color scheme.**

Balanced tension is often the nirvana of the stitching world. Getting top and bobbin threads to meet perfectly within a stitched piece takes adjustment work and fine-tuning. Often this job is left to the machine's "auto tension." However, relying on top tension adjustments does not always achieve desired results. Sometimes it is best to adjust the bobbin tension as well.

Using a test sample in the same materials as your project is recommended for most every sewing project including passport pages. On it, you can audition different thread choices as well as work towards that perfect tension.

Working with balanced tension is simply good technique. However, you can also stitch in a playfully unbalanced manner. By experimenting with top and bobbin tensions, you can achieve special effects and color bonuses. By bringing a second color of thread into your stitch line, you can add a layer of interest to your work.

Surprise colors can appear with top or bobbin sewing. Use different colors in the top and bobbin. If stitching from the top, raise the top tension to pull the bobbin thread up. When bobbin-sewing, lower the top tension to allow the needle thread to loop through to the bobbin-stitched side. In doing so, your line of stitches will feature two colors instead of one!

P.S. Try this technique with zigzag, patterned or free motion sewing.

PLAY WITH YOUR STITCHES

We learn by doing. We learn by experimenting. We learn by failing. The most beautiful and best-laid plans of the sewist are nothing until the sewing actually begins. If we are content to follow patterns and instructions forever, we will become proficient at the task. But, if we are willing to boldly play and chart personally new territory, we will begin to discover limitless potential.

By playing with our threads and stitches, we broaden our repertoire of choices. Choosing amongst and using these options will eventually become automatic and familiar. We encourage you to really get to know your machine and threads. Read the manual (yikes!). Make unfamiliar thread choices. The joy of play will not go unrewarded.

P.S. You can make numerous pages just playing with your machine's built in stitches.

The simple zigzag stitch can become a fluid wave of color by playing with its width and length as you stitch. Blend in waves of straight stitching. Try adding metallic threads for effect.

Satin stitches can often be elongated into bold, full lengths of color. The triple stitch can make a strong line. Play with your machine's pattern stitches. Try using a circular foot for curves. In this case, Rayon and Mirage threads were used.

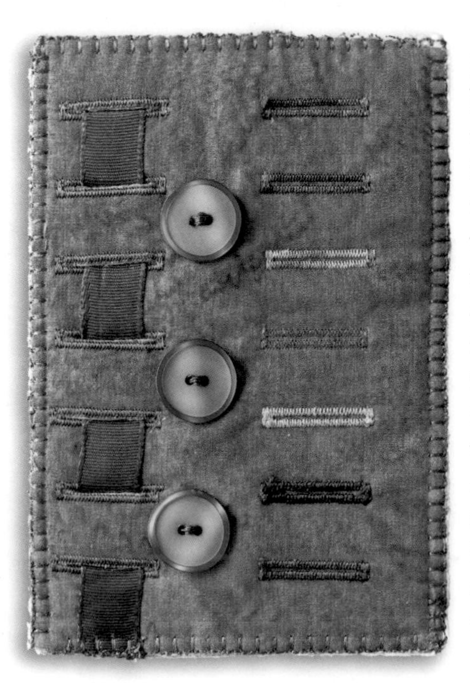

Buttonholes need not be stitched out of one type of thread. Before finishing a garment, try out different colors, weights and finishes of thread for effect. You can even stitch with two threads through the same needle (a size 14 or 16 topstitch works well for this). And buttonholes need not be strictly functional. They can also be used as an embellishment stitch.

Try out many of the specialty feet that are available for your machine. In this case, the tailor tacking (or fringe) foot was used for faggoting and fringing with metallic and rayon threads. The beading foot easily applies strung beads.

QUILT RELATED STITCHES

P.S. Quilting introduces us to a world of specialized stitches and techniques. Why not audition some of your stitches and thread choices on your pages?

Piecing/quilting

Make samples of piecing using InvisaFil, DecoBob and Silco. You can easily see the differences in the finished product. The old standard to match your thread to your fabric content might be necessary for a quilt that will be used on a bed or a garment that will be machine washed but may not apply for art quilts or home decorating projects. The bottom line is to use the thread that works best for your specific project.

Handwork

This passport page is a helpful visual aid for hand embroidery with Rayon, Accent, Razzle and Dazzle. Each thread is used in French knots, running stitch, and two different embroidery stitches. Through experimentation such as this you will find that WonderFil threads are exceptional for hand embroidery, as it isn't prone to tangling. We suggest using short lengths when using Dazzle.

Appliqué

Three different machine appliqué methods are shown here: raw edge, satin stitch, and blanket stitch. Each method lends a distinct style to your projects. You may also want to try an invisible appliqué using InvisaFil and a hemstitch.

Free form appliqué

Invisible isn't always better! This is a different breed of machine appliqué. Here the threads are the stars! Use a scribble stitch to attach the heart to the background and to accentuate the heart shape. Stitched with Mirage thread.

EDGE FINISHES

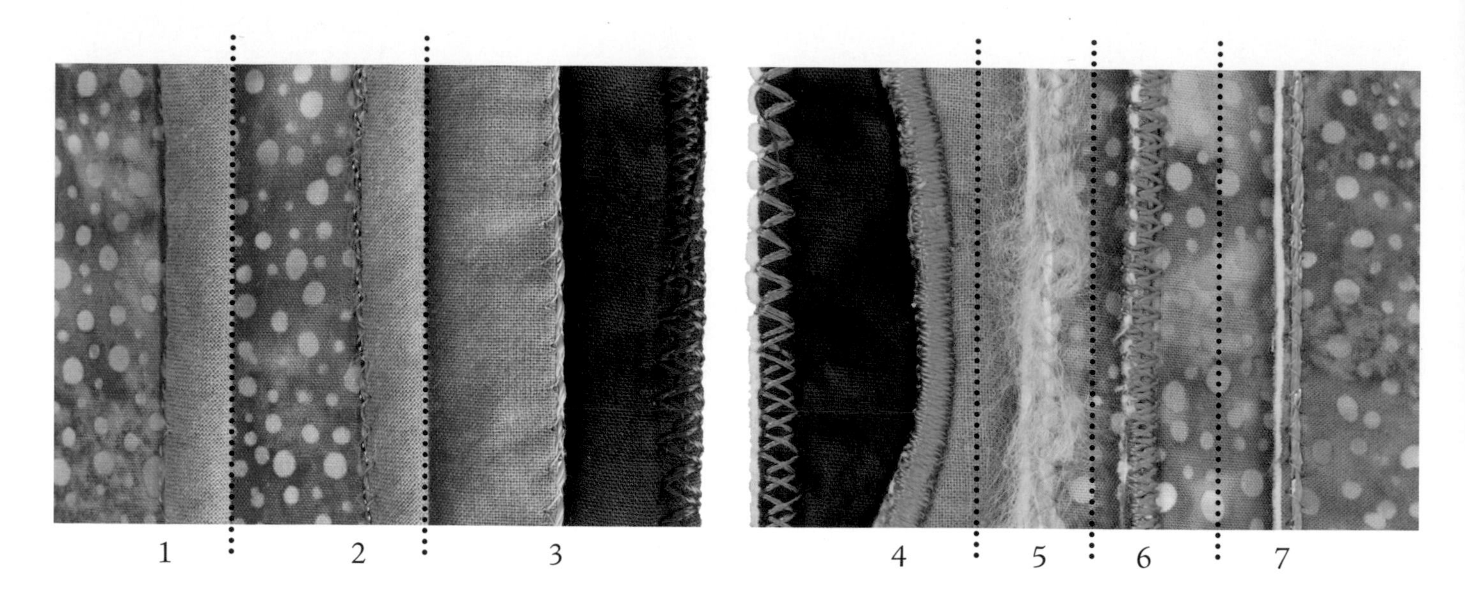

How many ways can you think of to finish the edge of a quilt? A visual sample can help make the right decision at the end of your project. Here are a few of the finishes we came up with. From left to right:

1. A traditional binding is sewn on the front of the quilt sandwich, pressed to the back and hand stitched.
2. A traditional binding is sewn on by machine. A strand of yarn is couched on top at the edge of the binding.
3. The quilt is finished right sides together and turned inside out through a small opening that is then hand stitched closed. For added interest, a strand of dazzle is couched to the edge.
4. This is a fun way to make a scalloped edge. Draw your scallop pattern on your fabric edge; do not cut yet. Straight stitch following your drawn lines all around the quilt. Adjust your machine to a zigzag stitch; use a shortened stitch length and a slightly narrowed width. Sew all the way around your quilt using the straight stitch line as a guide. Trim as close to the stitching as you can. Use tear-away stabilizer under the edge and using a wide satin stitch go over the entire top again. Remove the stabilizer and you have a great finish.
5. For this soft finish zigzag around the entire edge once then couch down a line of yarn.
6. A zigzag stitch is used to finish this edge. You need to go around the edge a couple times to ensure good coverage. You could use a tight zigzag or satin stitch if you prefer a neater edge.
7. Zigzag with DecoBob while couching over a length of Dazzle for a raw edge finish.

Be it for passports, postcards or art quilts, your edges need to be finished somehow. Why resort to a simple traditional binding when so many options abound? These are especially appropriate for quilts that will not be heavily used or washed.

P.S. The layout of this passport page looks complicated, but it is not. Each mini edge finish sample is finished on all sides. They are then layered from the outermost edge inward, tucking each successive mini page under the previous page's edge and stitching it in place on the outermost edge with a zigzag stitch. They are arranged in this way to avoid contact with the eyelet/buttonhole space.

FREE MOTION STITCHING

Free motion sewing is one of the best tools in the stitcher's toolbox of techniques. As its name implies, it offers an unparalleled freedom of sewing. If you can think it, you can most likely free motion stitch it! Quilting, thread painting, free-appliqué and thread writing. It is all possible with free motion sewing.

Most beginner sewists shy away from free motion because it can be tricky to learn. But so was walking. We stumbled many times, but soon mastered the technique and eventually ran! Free motion sewing takes practice. Practice not only makes you a better stitcher; it also helps you to develop your own stitching style. How liberating is it to discover that free motion does not just imply stipple stitching (and all of its associated 'rules')? You can not only meander and stipple, but you can also stitch in loops, turned squares, bubbles or vines. Your lines can indeed cross and you can use any thread that you choose!

Some guidelines to help you on your way:

1. Relax. Lower your shoulders. Loosen your neck and arms. Everything gets lowered, especially your own stress level!
2. Lower the feed dogs.
3. Lower machine tension a bit from normal settings.
4. Lower your needle into the 'needle down' position if you have this option. This way, the needle holds the fabric in position should you need to stop sewing.
5. Try DecoBob in the bobbin.
6. Try stitching with any WonderFil thread that you can fit through the needle.

P.S. Stitch out these pages as an introduction to your free motion options.

A Stippled Sampler in:

1. Metallic
2. Rayon
3. Deco-Bob
4. Mirage
5. Accent
6. D-Twist

Stitch Sampler
Rayon stitches beautifully with DecoBob or matching Rayon in the bobbin. Stitch intuitively. Wander where your needle takes you. Try new shapes, like loops or vines.

Variety
Don't limit yourself to straight stitching. Try zigzag free motion. Try a twin needle with either matching Rayon threads or contrasting colors. Hand-turn the needle through a few stitches to be sure that the needle will not strike the needle plate. Try two Rayon threads through one needle.

Trapunto
Easy stitched trapunto with InvisaFil in the needle and bobbin and two layers of batting beneath the fabric. First, free motion a heart shape. Then trim away one layer of batting around the outside edge of the heart. Continue stitching with a stipple stitch around the outside of the heart. Through the remaining one layer of batting and fabric.

There are no short-cuts to any place worth going.
~ Beverly Sills

HEAVY THREAD STITCHERY

WonderFil's extraordinary heavy threads are unlike any on the market. Razzle, Dazzle and Sizzle are equal in weight to size eight crochet cotton and they work beautifully either in the bobbin or couched under decorative stitches. They can also be used to great effect in hand stitching and embellishment. While Accent is also a heavy thread, 12 wt, it will fit through a larger needle and can thus be sewn from the top or the bobbin. All of these threads make a definite statement in texture and color. They sit atop the fabric rather than sink into it.

While it would seem that their heavy weight limits these threads to only decorative work, they can also be used for quilting and finishing edges. When combined with an underlying layer of anchoring stitches in InvisaFil or DecoBob, these heavy threads can add new dimension to your stitch techniques.

P.S. Wind a few bobbins with heavy thread and experiment!

Couching
Use a cording foot to tack one, two or three rows of heavy thread atop fabric. The heavy threads are held in place by small channels on the sewing foot while a wide decorative stitch such as a triple zigzag or serpentine stitch tack them in place. This stitch can be made with a coordinating rayon thread in a blending or accent color. It could also be stitched in InvisaFil or DecoBob for a more invisible finish. Yarns can be couched down with a beading or couching foot, which has a deeper channel to accommodate the fiber.

Bobbin Stitching
Free motion bobbin stitching takes a little bit of practice to get the tensions right. The bobbin tension can be bypassed on some machines, but if you can learn to adjust your bobbin tensions, you will have more options for your sewing. The goal is to pull the bobbin thread snug to the fabric. A loose bobbin tension allows the heavier bobbin threads to pass freely but not with enough tension to have them lay flat on the fabric. Tightening the upper tension serves to pull the upper thread snugly to the bobbin thread, holding it firmly in place. Try stitching straight and curved lines with all the different heavy threads in the bobbin. Using a blending color of DecoBob in the top thread makes it virtually invisible. A slightly lower tension with a contrasting Rayon thread in the top will allow both threads to show through on the finished side.

Stitch Patterns
With heavy threads in the bobbin, try stitching various machine stitch patterns. Some stitches work better than others, so try several. You can also try a Cornelli style stitch as seen in the looping pink and green threads. This stitch is achieved by using the triple straight stitch which may look like this on your machine: (--≡--).

Machine Sashiko with Accent
Sashiko style stitching is the traditional Japanese hand stitching that uses heavy white thread on indigo fabric. A stab stitch is used to follow a continuous line pattern where threads do not retrace the same line twice. Careful planning of your stitch path as well as a slightly lengthened stitch length and the counting of stitches can be used to achieve a very similar effect by machine using Accent thread through the needle. In this example, parallel lines are stitched one inch apart. A continuous angled line is then stitched from one line to the nex The number of stitches taken from the first line to the second i counted and that number is ther repeated to join each subsequent line. You can also achieve a sashiko style stitch using some built-in machine patterns.

Tip:
Here are three great reasons not to re-spool your thread:

1. It never gets wound back onto the spool with the same twist, which can cause tension and breakage problems.

2. Sewing machine technicians will tell you: simply grabbing the spool and pulling the thread backwards through the thread path and tension discs is not a good idea. Threads can snag, break off and cause unnecessary wear going backwards.

3. Saving all of your snipped threads makes the 'fill' for your thread structures. Keep a plastic bag or thread catcher nearby to collect all of your treasures!

Thread Cather by Michele Bremner

STITCHED POST CARDS

Postcards send a record of our travels to friends afar. Making and sending fabric postcards has become a worldwide phenomenon. Creating your passport pages gives you all of the experience that you need to make a fabric postcard. Your practice pieces just might impress you enough that you have to make copies to share with the world.

Thread work is an excellent way to embellish postcards. WonderFil's variety of threads gives you many options that will look fabulous and keep the postal system happy!

These are some simple guidelines for making your cards to mail:

1. Work with a **standard 4" x 6" size.**
2. **Stabilize or stiffen your card to make it firm enough for mailing.** You can use fast-2-fuse™, pelmet weight Vilene™, or similar products. You can also try card stock or watercolor paper. We stabilize each side of the card unless using a heavier product such as Timtex™.
3. How will you **finish the card's edge?** Complete each side of the card separately and then stitch and finish the edges similar to your passport pages. To address the cards, you can write on the fabric with fine point fabric markers, gel pens or rubber stamps. There are also many 'Post Card' rubber stamps. You can also print a label on fabric and fuse it to the card.
4. **Not too many embellishments!** Try to keep your embellishments and edge finishes flat, secure and not too bulky for the postal machines. After all, we want to keep our mail art flowing!

Little by little, one travels far.
~ JRR Tolkien

ArchiTexture

Summer Dreams Table Topper

Quilting

-(N) The stitches that hold a quilt together.
-(V) The act of stitching together the top, filling and back of a quilt.

ArchiTexture

-(N) The art and science of designing a structure of interwoven fibers or other elements.
-A fresh approach to considering the role which threads will play in your quilting.

In beginning to explore the wide variety of threads available from WonderFil and looking at the following suggested techniques, you may recognize some familiar approaches and fresh ideas. Some of these ideas may contradict the "rules of quilting" that you may have been taught. We have heard many of these rules and we respect their value in teaching and fine tuning proficient technique. However, we also believe that there is a need for respecting freedom of expression in your art. After all, you are the quilt maker, the designer and artist. You invest your time, effort and creative energies in your work. Quilt wherever your needle and thread take you. And if we may, we would like to respectfully submit that there is only one true rule in quilting:

"Make it so it doesn't fall apart."

THE EVOLUTION OF THREAD IN QUILTING

Lone Star by Allison Spence

Early in your stitch journey you may have been taught that quilting was to be "sensed and not seen." Quilting stitches were to be hidden in the ditch or made invisible around appliqué. They were to quietly offer a shadow of texture in machine stippling or hand sewing.

Quilting methods have multiplied to include the traditional methods while also allowing for the bolder use of the needle and thread. Quilters are exploring new interpretations of using threads and WonderFil can help them in their journey, no matter which path they choose to travel. Their variety of thread weights, colors and textures can meet the challenges of the traditional and the contemporary quilter.

The fine weights and subtle coloring of InvisaFil and DecoBob allow for subtle, supporting role stitching. They create the sense of invisible stitching without having to deal with the sheen, breakage or melting of some 'invisible' threads. Instead, their colors and minute stitch lines fall right into the fabric.

Silco cotton thread provides the delicate matte finish of cotton thread without the lint. Available in soft solid colors as well as vibrant variegated colors to meet the needs of many quilters, this thread is suitable for machine and hand stitching. It also works well as a top stitching thread and it looks great on denim quilts.

The sheen of rayon threads catches and reflects the light. When using Rayon or Mirage threads, color and light recedes and advances across your quilt. The transition between colors in the Mirage thread is subtle and when it is used in stippling, the stitches appear to be floating and free flowing. An additional benefit to quilting with this variegated thread is that it tends to be forgiving of less than 'perfect' stitching.

Special effects can be achieved when using the Hologram and Metallic collections for quilting. Metallic threads can heat up when passing through the many metal parts of your machine. This can cause friction. It sometimes helps to bypass the final thread guide on your machine and to stitch at a slightly slower speed when using these threads.

The bold colors and texture of Accent thread can make for dramatic stitching. Whether using it with a straight stitch and a walking foot or in free motion, this thread will definitely get your quilting noticed!

Three Rising by Loraine Kreznar

INTERVIEW WITH A QUILTER

Marcie Lane is a national award winning quilter. She creates original designs as well as patterned quilts. Her work runs the gamut from traditional to contemporary to experimental. She has made over 300 quilts! We asked Marcie about her quilting experience and her thoughts on WonderFil's assorted threads:

Raven's Crest

"I discovered WonderFil Specialty Threads a few years ago. I love patchwork quilting, hand and machine appliqué, hand and machine piecing, free motion quilting, and I even play with art quilts when I have time. I also use these threads for beading both by hand and machine. Okay, there isn't much that I haven't done in quilting!"

"I love InvisaFil thread. This is truly invisible thread! It comes in a wide range of colors and is easy to handle, unlike other 'invisible' threads on the market. It isn't shiny and you can iron it with no problems. My quilt, Raven's Crest (The Great Canadian Quilt Challenge 2004, Honorable Mention), was entirely stitched with InvisaFil, including the hand appliqué. I know in some areas of quilting it's all about seeing the thread, but it's also true that in some areas of quilting it's all about NOT seeing the thread!"

"Silco lint-free cotton is another favorite of mine. I use it for machine piecing, quilting and hand piecing. Rayon Embroidery is wonderful for satin stitch appliqué as well as thread painting. Deco Bob is a multipurpose thread that I use for piecing, machine quilting and appliqué as well."

"The Yin Yang sample shows the symbols in hand appliqué, invisible machine appliqué, blanket stitch and satin stitch appliqué. I used InvisaFil for the hand and invisible appliqué. I used Silco for the blanket stitch appliqué and Rayon Embroidery for the satin stitch. I free motion stipple quilted the black areas with my machine using black InvisaFil. For the red areas, I used red Rayon Embroidery thread."

Yin Yang

When asked if she had any tips for using WonderFil threads, Marcie responded:

"It's important to use the proper needle designed for specific threads. Don't be afraid to adjust your top tension. And, don't forget to experiment and have fun!"

QUILTING OUT OF THE DITCH

Quilting in the ditch is a tried and true method for quilting. Here are some ideas for alternate methods to try.

Channel Quilting is stitching in parallel lines. InvisaFil or Deco Bob stitch a fine line. Color choice can either blend in with the background fabric or be a highlight color that might pick up on other elements in the quilt.

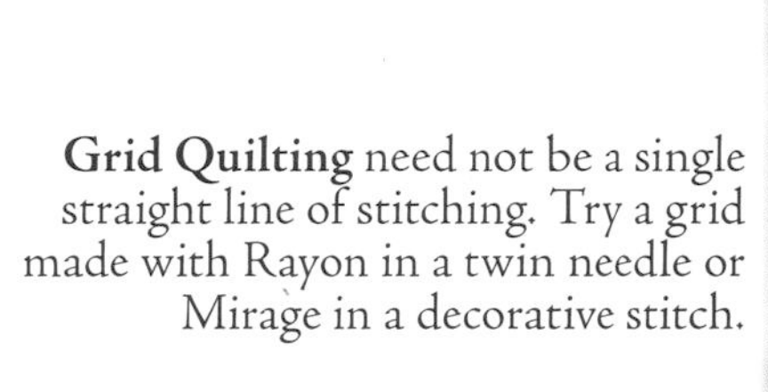

Grid Quilting need not be a single straight line of stitching. Try a grid made with Rayon in a twin needle or Mirage in a decorative stitch.

Waves and Lines are a breeze to stitch but can have great impact with the right thread. Try layers of different colors and even add a bit of sparkle with Metallic or Hologram thread. These lines can be stitched with a walking foot or in free motion.

Geometric Pivots made with Accent thread are easy-to-stitch bursts of color either on their own or echoing border or appliqué shapes.

Block Cues: Take your stitching cues from your pieced patterns. Stitch over the ditch with a machine pattern, or turn the stitching on point. Echo the patterns with boldly stitched lines in your setting squares.

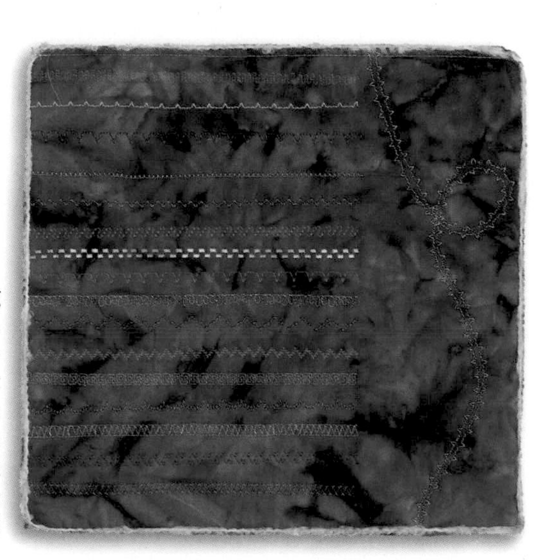

Pattern Stitches with a walking foot? Check your machine's manual. If the walking foot balks with pattern stitching anchor stitch first with a line of InvisaFil and then over stitch with a colorful pattern in Rayon, Mirage or Silco with an all-purpose foot. Using less complex patterns can be quite effective!

P.S. Why not explore some of these suggestions using passport sized mini quilts?

SUMMER DREAMS TABLE TOPPER

This project is a great way to use a seemingly unrelated group of fabrics for a fun, eclectic look. The various threads used in the quilting tie the fabrics together.

Supply List:
Assorted Plaids—scraps are fine
¼ yard (0.25m) of inner border fabric
1¾ yards (1.60m) of outer border fabric
4 yards (3.66m) of backing fabric or consider using scraps pieced together
5-7 colors solid and/or variegated Silco picking up colors from the different plaids
InvisaFil, DecoBob or Silco for piecing
Tear-away stabilizer
Quilt batting, for this project a flat batting is preferred
Walking foot or even feed foot

Directions:

1. Cut assorted plaids into 4½" (11.5cm) squares.
   You will need 49 squares.
   Cut 4 inner border strips 1" (2.5cm) wide
   Cut 5 outer border strips 11" (28cm) wide
2. Piece the plaid squares together using traditional quilt piecing methods. It is helpful to lay out all the squares first to ensure a pleasing pattern. Press carefully to have the seams lay as flat as possible. Add your borders and press flat again.
3. Piece your backing fabric to achieve the necessary size for your quilt. Lay it out on a flat surface right side down taping down the edges to keep the backing taut. Lay batting on top of wrong side of backing fabric, smoothing out bumps and ripples. Lay quilt top on the batting. Square up the top by measuring from corner to corner in both directions; these measurements should match. If they don't match, tug on the quilt top to square it up. Baste quilt layers together using your favorite basting method.
4. Here comes the fun part. You may choose to use the same or different threads in the bobbin depending on your backing fabric and the look you prefer. Start with one of your Silco threads and using the walking foot quilt in gently wavy lines diagonally across the quilt from corner to corner. Move to the opposite corner and repeat. (*Figure 1*) Move out from the first lines about 4" (10cm) and repeat the wavy quilting using the first line of stitching as a rough guide. When you get to the opposite edge simply turn the quilt ¼ turn and begin again. (*Figure 2*) Continue in this pattern until you run out of bobbin thread. Each time you change bobbins change the upper thread color and give the quilt a thorough pressing. Pressing often helps keep the quilt flat. After you have quilted around the entire quilt once, go around again filling in the spaces between your first round of stitching. (*Figure 3*) For your third time around the quilt begin quilting in the remaining spaces but this time begin to let your lines cross each other (see detail photograph above). Continue until you are happy with the amount of quilting.

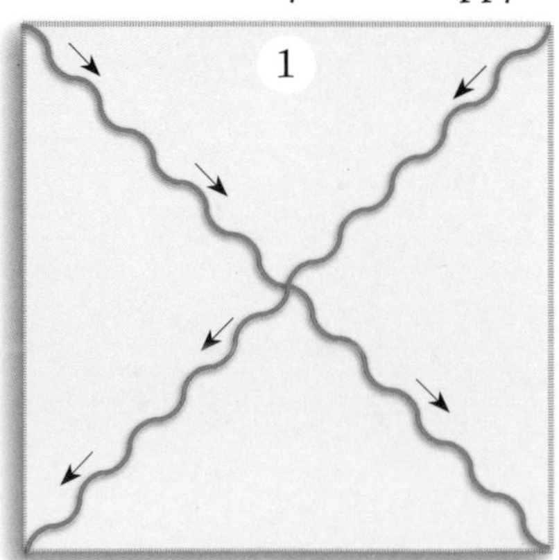

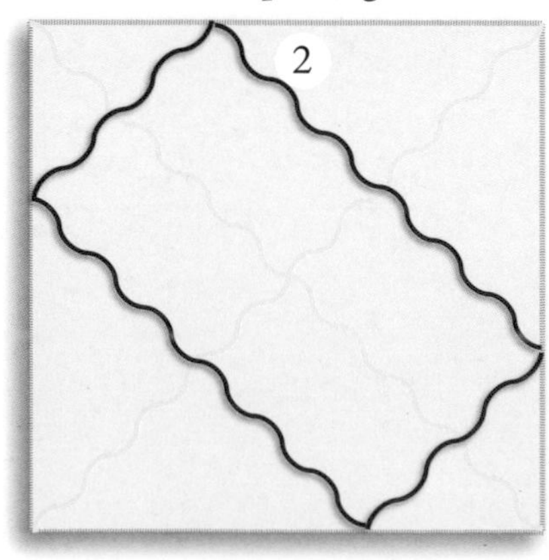

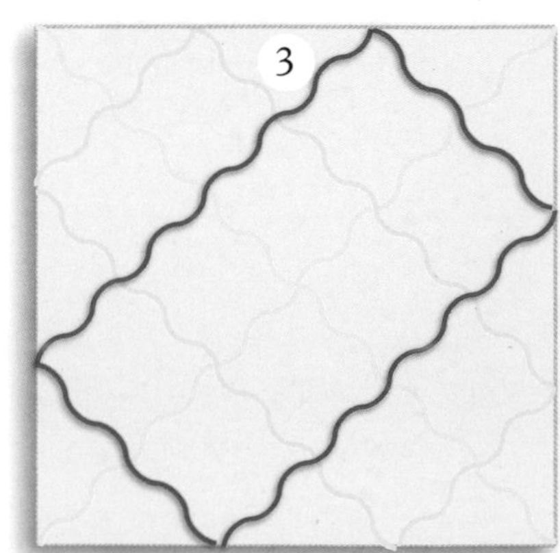

5. For a fun edge finish, try a satin stitched scalloped border like the one in the "edge finish" passport page. Draft your scallop pattern on freezer paper. Divide the length of the quilt by the number of scallops you want. For example, Summer Dreams has 7 scallops with rounded corners but you may prefer 5 or 9 scallops. Subtract ½ of your scallop diameter from each edge and mark that spot. Summer Dreams scallop diameter is 5" half of that equals 2.5". Measure the distance between these two marks and cut your freezer paper this length. Mark the middle point of the template and make guide marks out to each edge the same distance apart as your scallop diameter (Summer Dreams is 5") and using a plate or compass, draw your scallops adjusting to fit as necessary. Iron the freezer paper to your top and use it as a template to mark your quilt. Remove freezer paper and re-iron on the next side and draw your pattern. Use the plate or compass to continue the curve around the corners. After you have drawn the pattern on the entire top remove the freezer paper and sew a straight stitch line along the drawn scallop edge. Then, using the straight stitch line as your guide, use a zigzag stitch around the entire quilt. Use a normal zigzag width with a fairly close but not satin stitch length (between a ½ and 1 stitch length). After you have gone around the entire top, trim the excess fabric close to the stitch line and press. Set your machine for a wide width zigzag and satin stitch length. Place 4" strips of tear-away stabilizer on the back of the quilt so that the line of stitching (the edge of the quilt) is in the middle of the stabilizer. Use the satin stitch around the edge of the quilt. When you are finished tear away the stabilizer and you are ready for your final press, a bottle of wine, crusty bread and Brie.

LONGARM QUILTING

Lisa Thiessen, www.threadsinmotion.ca

Lisa takes longarm quilting into new territory using metallic threads. When working with the metallic on top and DecoBob or InvisaFil in the bobbin, she likes to loosen the bobbin screw until there is just a tiny bit of tension on that thread. She also finds that bypassing the first thread guide, using a vertical spool pin and lightly wrapping a Wonder-Guard wrap around the metallic thread, all keep the thread running smoothly. Lisa also quilts "in-the-ditch" around the blocks using Silco.

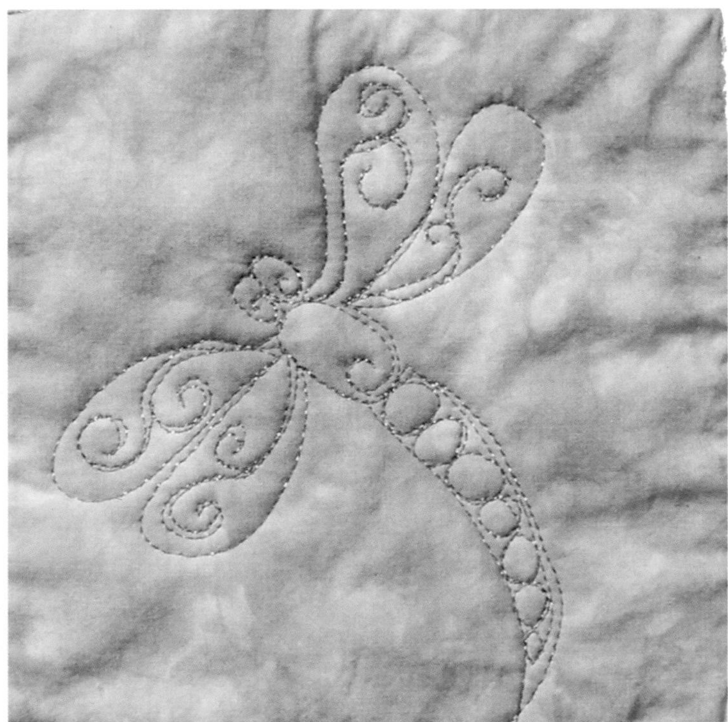

QUILT GALLERY

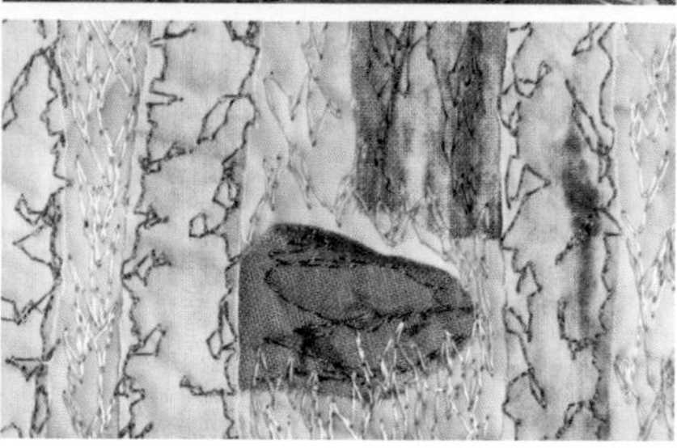

Cretan Labyrinth
By Loraine Kreznar

Inspired by ancient labyrinth designs this art quilt uses fused appliqué techniques with a decorative stitch as well as reverse appliqué. The simple fused design gets an added sense of movement with the use of a variegated thread. A combination of Silco and Rayon threads was used.

Spring Grove
By Loraine Kreznar

The essence of a spring hike in the mountains is captured in this appliqué art quilt. Thread work gives dimension and texture to the tree trunks, rocks and meadow grasses. Silco, Rayon and Mirage threads were used.

Crazy Quilt
By Jan Routh
Crazy quilting is an excellent opportunity to explore stitch and color. WonderFil's variety of thread weights and colors offers endless options to explore. The Rayon collection gives a fantastic sheen to your work and is wonderful to use in hand embroidery.

Thread as Paint

thread painted ***Pear Pillow***

The activity of painting: a thrilling tussle between the artist's materials and (her) inspiration.
~ Mervyn Levy

Every canvas is a journey all its own.
~ Helen Frankenthaler

As a thread artist, you wield not a brush, but a needle and from that needle flows your thread onto your canvas. By applying different amounts of color, line and texture, you can doodle, draw, paint and write with your thread.

DOODLE, DRAW, PAINT

Doodle- Akin to free motion embroidery, doodling usually gets stitched as a continuous line of repeating or random shapes. Your lines can cross. Think doodles from your school notebooks.

Draw- Often a continuous line of stitching but more pictorial in nature than free-motion doodles. You can draw still lifes, portraits, landscapes or anything that captures your interest. You can use more than one thread, but this isn't the place for heavy stitching. Stabilizer may be necessary. You may choose to fill in your stitching with colored pencils or paints.

Paint- Layers of color can be laid down with a heavy application of threads. Use a strong needle (size 14 or 16) and stabilizer. Often times thread painting is too heavy to stitch directly on your finished piece because it causes too much distortion. Instead, it is worked separately from the base fabric and treated as an appliqué. In this case, the thread painting can be stitched on water-soluble stabilizer, or stabilized fabric or tulle. Tulle or netting makes great bases because they add little bulk and the edges disappear when trimmed.

P.S. The garden is an easy place to get your inspiration for drawing. Give it a try. What is the worst that can happen? Really?

P.S. Stabilize a page and 'paint' with a variety of thread types and colors. See how stitching one over the other blends colors.

THREAD APPLIQUÉ

P.S. Your Passport Cover is a great place to try your hand at thread appliqué. We used a flying heart motif, but you can work out any design that strikes your desire. Since you are building up heavy layers of thread, you might try a heavier needle like a size 16 topstitch.

This is the method that we use:

- Draw an outline for your appliqué on paper.
- Trace this drawing onto heavy weight water soluble stabilizer.
- Lay the stabilizer over a piece of tulle and hoop both of these layers together.
- Set up your machine for free motion.
- Outline stitch your motif, then retrace this outline several times.
- Change colors and fill in your design. Repeat as needed.
- Your sewing will sound rough as your appliqué is nearly finished.
- Trim carefully around your design and rinse away the stabilizer if necessary.
- Stitch in place with light stitching in the center portion of the design in a blending color and then around the perimeter, as this helps to keep the appliqué flat.

THE PEAR PILLOW

Rubber-stamping can help to provide an easy to stitch motif. It can also give you a consistent design when you wish to repeat an image. In this case, a pear stamp from ***Stampers Anonymous*** was used.

Stamping on Fabric:

- Use an ink based stamp pad such as ***Tsukineko*** brand's ***Fabrico***™ (or ***Versacolor***™).
- Press fabric flat. To stabilize it more, you may want to apply a temporary stabilizer to the back of the fabric such as freezer paper.
- Use a clean, deeply etched stamp. Lay it right side up in one hand and hold the stamp pad in the other. Lightly 'tap-tap-tap' the ink all over the stamp.
- Carefully center the stamp on the fabric. Apply an even pressure without 'rocking' the stamp. We often will use the covered stamp pad to press down on the stamp.
- When lifting the stamp, hold a corner of the fabric with one hand and lift the pad with the other to prevent the fabric from lifting up with the stamp.
- Allow the ink to dry before ironing or hasten the process with a heat gun.

Shaded Thread Painting of the Pears:

Threads used: Very light–medium–very dark shades of one 'pear' color, D-Twist for background.

- Fuse paper backed fusible web (or use a stabilizer of choice) behind fabric that is larger than the stamp and big enough to fit in your hoop.
- Stamp the image as above & hoop the fabric.
- Begin by stitching the main color of the pear in medium Rayon embroidery thread.
- Fill in the background around the pear with D-Twist (adds a multicolored, textured background).
- Selectively stitch light and dark areas with the light and dark threads. More detail can be achieved with a greater variety of values, but this is simple and effective.
- Thread writing is used to stitch *Les Trois Petites Poires*, French for *The Three Little Pears*.
- Trim, fuse and appliqué in place on the front of your favorite pillow pattern.

THE PAINTED DAISY TOTE

This tote bag is a great way to start playing with thread painting using digital photographs or rubber-stamped images to help those less than confidant in their drawing skills. You can create fabulous and unique embroidery designs without an expensive embroidery machine.

Supplies:

Printed photo image of flowers or rubber-stamped flower image
Assorted fabrics to match your color choices
Variegated Rayon and Accent threads
Your favorite tote bag pattern or design your own
Fusible web such as Steam-a-seam™ or Wonder Under™
Tear away stabilizer such as Stitch N Tear™
Heavyweight stabilizer such as Fast2Fuse™, Timtex™ or Pellon Craft fuse™
Machine embroidery hoop
Size 90/14 embroidery needle for your machine

Directions:

1. Adjust the colors of a digital photograph in your photo software and print out on fabric. Or if you aren't comfortable with digital printing choose a large single flower rubber stamp and simply stamp out your flower image.

2. To set up your flower for embroidery, pin your image on the tear-away stabilizer and place in your hoop. It is often helpful to use two layers of stabilizer. Beginning with your chosen variegated rayon thread, outline the flower petals as well as the center. Once this first round is finished you may remove any pins. Start filling in the individual flower petals. Begin from the edge of the flower center; stitch out to the end of the petal and back following the contour of the petal. Refer to the passport pages below for detailed photos. It is more effective to make a few stitches in each petal going around the entire flower multiple times rather than fill in one petal at a time. Otherwise, using the variegated thread you end up with one light petal and one dark petal rather than a mix in each petal. Continue around the flower until it is as full as you like. Relax and have fun, if a line of stitch is outside the flower shape don't fret. It is part of the casual, easy feel of this painting technique.

3. Embroider the flower center using a coordinating Accent thread. Stitch the area using small circular stitching until the center is full.

4. Press with steam or use a spray bottle to dampen the embroidery and iron to flatten out your stitching. Trim to the desired size. Occasionally small areas of the background fabric will draw up. Generally they can be pressed out so they are not noticeable. If your background fabric is extremely distorted, don't despair. Simply make your flower a stand-alone appliqué by cutting it out from the fabric. An edge of Accent thread makes a great border. Try the technique again after adjusting your tension.

5. To assemble the blocks for the front of the tote bag use either traditional quilt piecing techniques or the raw edge fusing technique that was used on the Painted Daisy Tote. Raw edge fusing is a more imperfect technique than traditional piecing. Cut or tear your fabric in strips the approximate size you would like in your block. Lay a piece of fusible webbing cut to your block sizes on your work surface fusible side up. Position your fabric strips and appliqué flower in an arrangement that is pleasing to you. With this technique you can successfully overlap areas without the need for set-in seams by the addition of a bit more fusible webbing under the fabrics. Be careful to slightly overlap your fabrics instead of butting them together so that none of the background stabilizer shows through. When you are satisfied with your block arrangements use your iron to fuse it together. When all the blocks for your piece are finished, fuse them to your heavyweight stabilizer. If the heavyweight stabilizer you are using for your bag form is fusible skip this step and make your blocks directly on the heavyweight stabilizer.

6. Now it's time to embellish your blocks. If you used the raw edge fusing technique you need to first stitch some basic stitching lines along the edges of the fabrics to ensure they don't delaminate over time. Once these are done, it's time to doodle! In the Painted Daisy piece I used a variety of threads as well as stitches to embellish the blocks; garnet stitch, free motion stitching, grid stitching, and simple straight-line stitch. Add trims, beads, feathers or yarns. The sky is the limit.

7. Finish your bag according to your pattern, if you are using one, or design one yourself that will meet your exact needs.

WRITING WITH YOUR THREAD

Lettering on fabric can be done free hand or guided by pre-printed templates made from disappearing stabilizers. These are some of the methods that we use for free-motion lettering:

- Handwrite on water-soluble stabilizer with a fine fabric marker. Lay the water-soluble film atop fabric and either freely stitch or hoop the fabric and stabilizer and stitch over the lettering. Try practicing the motions of your writing on paper first (without sewing). This "warm-up" gets your hands limbered up for the motions that you will be stitching in.
- Use your ink jet printer to print onto water-soluble paper (that will lie atop fabric) or directly onto pretreated printable fabric. There are many computer fonts that look fabulous when stitched. Play with the size and variety of these to find your favorites.
- Trace printed lettering onto water-soluble (such as newspaper headlines).
- Rubber stamp letters directly onto fabric and stitch over them.
- Use your embroidery machine fonts.

P.S. Sample different writing methods. We tried printed, water-soluble paper working on water-soluble film and stitching over stamped design.

SWEET DREAMS PILLOW

The Sweet Dreams Pillow was created with a photo printed on fabric and appliquéd to the linen base fabric using a decorative machine stitch in Rayon over ribbon. The words "sweet dreams' were printed on a wash-away stabilizer and then machine stitched over the printing. The printing was done in a color close to the thread color. Buttons were stitched on using D-Twist that was casually frayed for a soft detail.

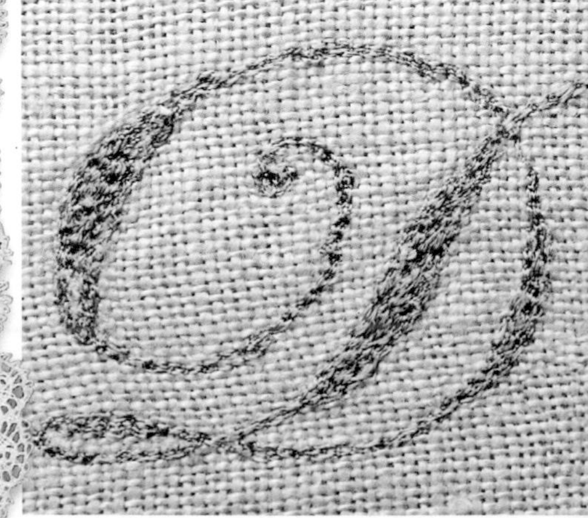

Froggy See, Froggy...
By Jan Routh

This enchanting pond image is a wonderful example of thread used as a stand-alone appliqué. The frog, dragonfly, fish and leaves are all worked on dissolvable stabilizer then appliquéd to the art quilt top. Rayon and Mirage threads were used.

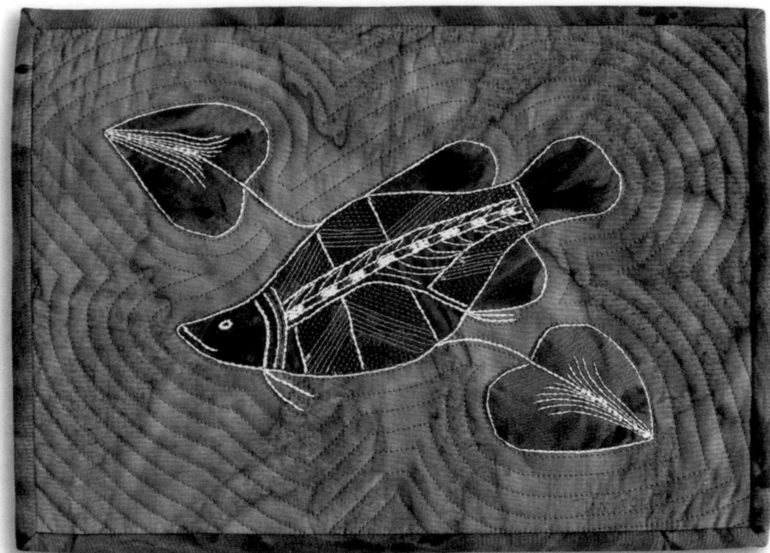

Barramundi
By Jan Routh

The transformation of plain fabric to art is as simple as applying thread. This Barramundi is inspired by Australian Aboriginal artwork. The echo quilting enhances the feel of the fish swimming in his native seas. All rayon threads are used in this art quilt.

Floral Felt Purse
By Gordana Brelih

Free style flowers were heavily stitched on water-soluble stabilizer using a wide variety of colors in Rayon Embroidery thread. The stabilizer was then dissolved and the flowers were appliquéd to the front of this simple-yet-elegant purse made of felt. Note the stitching detail that wraps around the purse handle.

Thread as Structure

In dimensional threadwork, thread becomes the delicate textile that can be formed and molded into a structure. The primary step in creating structure with threads is stitching in regular, criss-crossing grids. The strength of these creations depends on their interlocking components and how they are stabilized.

Thread vase, machine embroidered bowl, thread bowl/votive holder and bookmark.

DIMENSIONAL THREADWORK

While two and three-dimensional thread structures may appear very different, they are built in the same manner. All of the techniques involve stitching on some type of stabilizer to form a thread grid fabric. You need to consider how your project will be made or used when deciding on the best stabilizer to use. Types of stabilizers include:

Disappearing- Water-soluble film (these come in light, medium and heavy weights), and heat disappearing fabric.

Disintegrating- These base stabilizers will break down or distort with heat or water, but they generally leave remnants behind. Examples include Tyvek™, felt, nylon organza, cellophane, or tissue paper.

Delicate- These are lightweight fabrics that act as base fabrics for your stitching. They remain in the project, but mostly act as something to create the stitch grid on. Examples include silk organza, tulle, netting, bubble wrap or brown paper.

Often, a thread grid will include "filler." This filler can be lightweight additions that will help build the grid more quickly and stronger. The bits often add interest to the thread grid fabric. Filler bits can be thread snips, yarn, Angelina® Fibers, silk bits or paper pieces. Take note that these are all lightweight so as not to weigh down the thread grid.

P.S. Try stitching various styles of grids. Stitch with different weights of threads. Stitch on different types of stabilizers. Stitch in any style, as long as threads interconnect.

P.S. Try stitching on different types of stabilizers: Disappearing (water-soluble), disintegrating (heat stressed organza), and delicate stabilizers (tulle).

CONSTRUCTION TECHNIQUES

The steps for a 2 – 3 D thread object are generally the same from project to project:

1. **Layering-** Make a sandwich of: stabilizer – filler – stabilizer.
2. **Marking-** If you need to mark your grid to have a guide you can draw it on your soluble stabilizer with a fine marker.
3. **Thread choice-** What do you want to stitch your grid with? Will you see both sides of the grid (as with a bowl)? Matching threads or contrasting colors should be considered as well as thread weight. Heavy threads in the bobbin help to build a grid more quickly, so Razzle, Dazzle or Sizzle may be a great choice. Accent on both sides form a heavy, bold line very easily.
4. **Hooping or pinning-** Secure your layers before you start stitching to avoid puckering and keep filler in place.
5. **Grid sewing-** Begin by stitching an anchoring grid. This would be your first run through the grid to hold it all in place, and then you could remove pins to move more freely. Retrace the grid several times and add stitches in between as desired.
6. **Constructive Sewing-** If pieces will be assembled as with a vase or box, try to stitch as many pieces together as possible BEFORE removing the stabilizer.
7. **Trimming-** Trim away excess stabilizer and threads before rinsing or burning it away as it is easier to trim a shape while it is still stabilized.
8. **Removing stabilizer-** Rinse or heat-treat stabilizer to breakdown or remove it. For pieces made with water-soluble stabilizer: only partially rinse away the film until the thread grid feels 'slick,' as this gooey residue is the liquid glue that will dry and help a shape to retain its form.

For pieces made with water-soluble stabilizer:

9. **Forming/Shaping-** Flat items can just lay flat on parchment paper to dry. For items such as bowls, you will need to drape the wet thread grid over a form and let it dry. Cover any form that you use with parchment paper or plastic wrap so as not to glue the grid to the form!
10. **Drying-** Allow the shape to dry for 24 hours. Forcing it to dry is not advisable, but if necessary a low setting on a heat gun can be used. Ironing is not recommended as a drying method because it flattens the fibers.
11. **Reshaping-** Should a shape not turn out as expected, it can be reshaped. Saturate the piece with water, and add pieces of water-soluble film. Partially dissolve the film into the piece by rinsing water through it. Once the piece is again slick and 'gooey,' reshape it over a bowl or other form.
12. **Seal-** An optional step is to spray the completely dried piece with a clear-coat spray sealer. Several coats will help harden the surface of the thread piece.

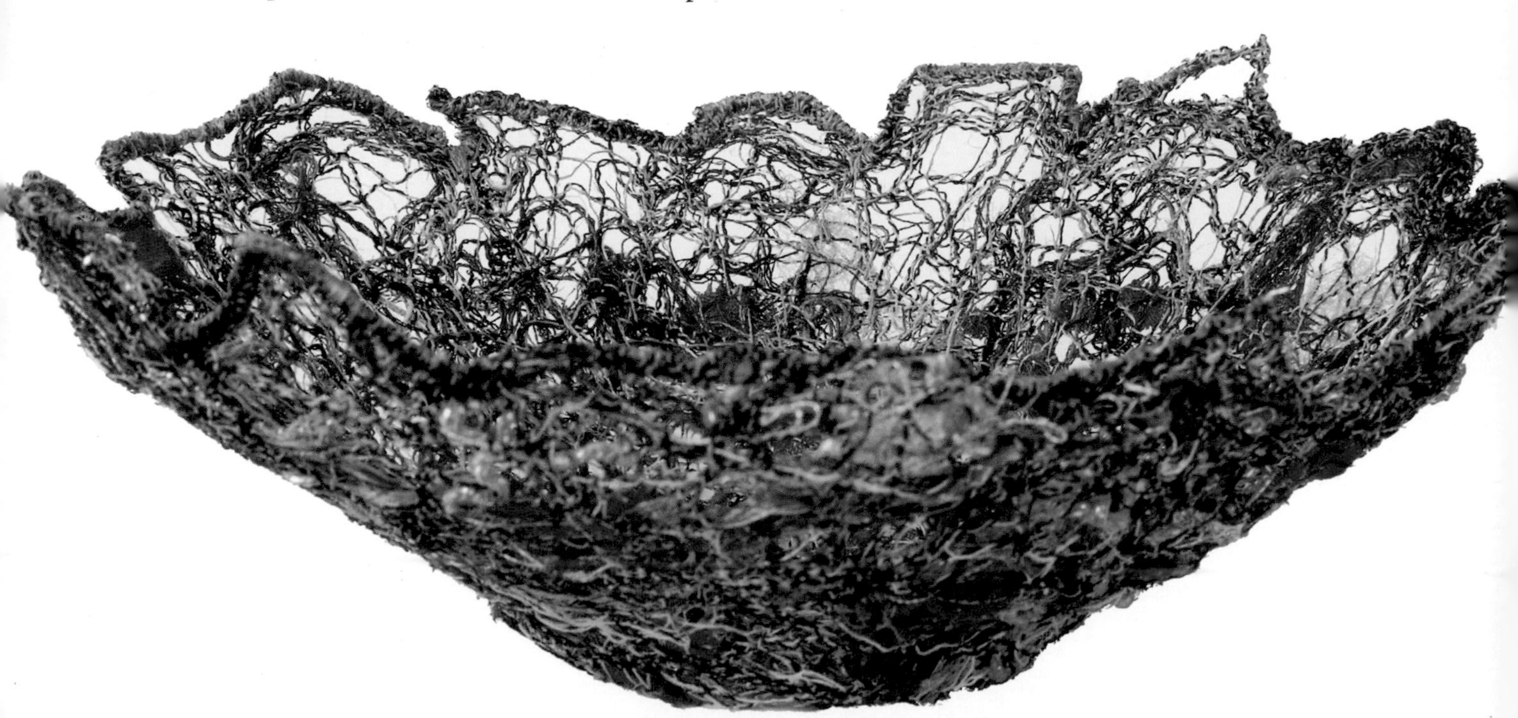

Bookmark- Two-dimensional pieces are dried flat. They can be made from a larger thread grid fabric that is cut randomly and applied as an embellishment (see remnants and shrine). For a bookmark, a piece can be trimmed to approximately 1½" x 7" by first marking a cutting line on the stitched grid and trimming it to size. Before rinsing away the stabilizer, stitch a tight zigzag around the perimeter to finish off the edge. Dry flat and add a tassel.

Votive Holder or Bowls- The thread grid fabric can be roughly trimmed in a circle that is large enough to drape over a glass votive holder or bowl. It can also be neatly finished with a zigzag or a couched fiber if desired. Once the stabilizer is mostly rinsed away, it can then be formed over a votive holder or bowl.

Machine Embroidered Bowl- A built-in quilting design on Janome's MC11000 using Accent thread and stitched over silk organza with metallic thread filler bits is easily turned into a bowl.

Thread Vase- The vase requires a larger piece of thread grid fabric. Enlarge the vase templates to 200%, then trace and cut four of the vase sides and one bottom. Zigzag finish the perimeter. Zigzag the four side-seams together, trapping a length of fine wire in each seam for stability. Rinse the stabilizer away and stand the form to dry over a wrapped box or cylinder. Once dry, attach the bottom piece with hand stitching to complete the vase. If you leave extra lengths of wire at the top, you can bead these.

Grid Embellishments- This fabric shrine is embellished with thread grids that have been cut and stitched in place.

REMNANTS

Remnants are assembled on artists' canvas (available in all sizes as boards or stretched). They are collections of what might look like left over bits from your stitching: torn bits of thread grids, delicately stabilized stitching, stitched ribbons. All of these can be blended together along with rubber-stamped sentiments and embellishments. Hence, the remnants of your work become reborn into a new piece.

Tips:

- Pre-paint canvas with assorted Lumiere paints.
- When rinsing water-soluble away, pat it dry and place it on the canvas. The remaining stabilizer will act as glue and bond it in place.
- Pre-stitch other bits and glue them in place for a 'stitched' look.

Thread as Ornament

A thread of history

Before there was fabric, there was thread. Sewing with a needle and thread dates back 30,000 years when the first threads were thin strips of animal hide. Thread used as ornament peaked during the Middle Ages when the art of tapestries took center stage. The next big advances for thread were during the Industrial Revolution when high-speed machines could produce stronger threads cheaply. For centuries, with the exception of the brief but glorious Victorian era, the use of thread in quilting, home decorating and clothing design has been more of an afterthought, just the lowly material that holds the fabulous fabrics together. Today, we are on the brink of a thread revolution. Gone are the days when black, white and gray threads would satisfy the home sewer. Would one ask Van Gogh or Monet to have only 3 or 6 paint colors at their disposal? In this chapter you will see ways to let your WonderFil threads shine. You will learn how they can totally change the look of a fabric, enhance clothing, or decorate paper.

Pictured above: *Wands of many Wonders*

MAKE YOUR OWN FABRIC

An ordinary fabric becomes extraordinary when it is remade with thread. Plain fabrics suddenly have a pattern, texture or added color. Patterned fabrics that we may no longer care for can be radically changed with all-over stitching. These techniques are easy-to-do, but offer great effect.

Use any of these techniques to make your own fabric (MYOF). Stitching is usually done before the fabric is cut into a pattern.

P.S. These pages are made similar to the edge finish pages. Completing eight different samples and finishing their edges with a zigzag stitch shows multiple techniques. These are then layered and stitched on two passport pages for a dimensional sampler.

Tip: When making your own fabric, start with a larger base fabric to allow for shrinkage. Stabilizer and lots of pressing will help to keep the fabric flat.

1. **Tufts** - Lay four strands of Razzle or Dazzle across the fabric. Use a wide zigzag in Rayon thread to tack them in place at regular intervals. Turn the fabric 90° and zigzag over previous stitches. This keeps the strands from pulling out. Snip away extra Razzle between tufts.
2. **Couching** - Couch Razzle at regular intervals to form an all over geometric grid.
3. **Patterned Rows** - Combine rows of assorted machine patterns stitched in Rayon.
4. **Diamonds** - Use a triple stitch to stitch a grid of diamonds in Rayon. Or use a straight stitch of Accent for an equally thick line.
5. **Box Pivots** - These do not have to be made with free-motion. Stitch with your needle down and pivot regularly to form boxes. Try using Mirage or variegated Silco.
6. **Twin Needle** - Parallel lines of Rayon stitches are easily achieved using a twin needle.
7. **Waves** - Use a walking or all-purpose foot to stitch multicolored waves with Silco.
8. **Spirals** - Free motion doodles in variegated Silco.

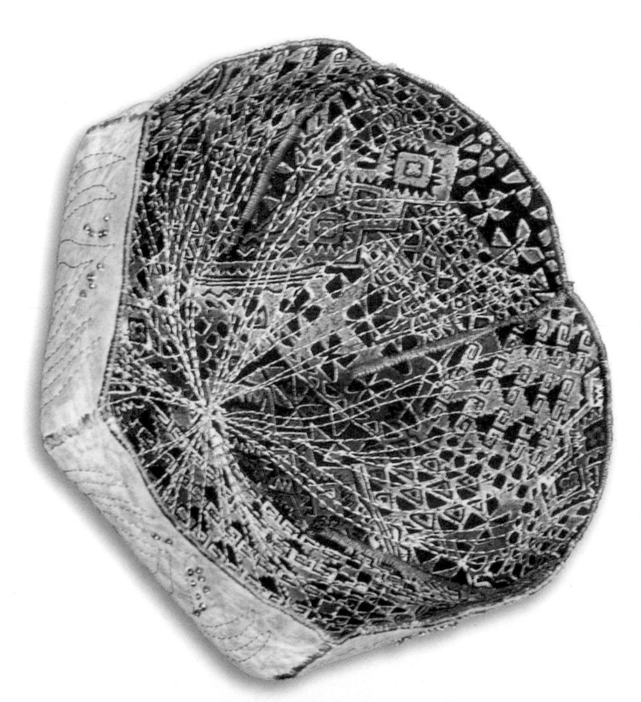

Reversible Bowl
Loraine Kreznar

In this original design, the strongly patterned interior fabric is altered with the heavy application of Accent thread. Accent's strong color and heavy texture effectively soften the appearance of the fabric to allow it to work in harmony with the bowl's exterior.

WANDS OF MANY WONDERS

We love to stitch, but sometimes we just want to play and not tend to life's distractions. Enter these magical wands that come together quickly and can be used to channel positive energies to vanquish any challenge!

Choose a theme for your wand. Some suggestions: Magic, Serenity, Believe, Enough Time, Good Health, Mess-No-More!, Creativity Conjurer... you get the idea!

The steps to making your wand:

1. Pre-stitch front and back fabrics that are larger than the star template in a MYOF style of choice.
2. Create your puffy stars using one of two methods:
   A. Turned Star:
      - Draw a star shape onto the wrong side of the front fabric. Lay front and back fabrics right sides together and stitch around the star twice, leaving a one-inch gap at the bottom for turning and stuffing.
      - Trim within 1/8 inch of the stitch line and turn right side out. Poke out the points of the stars.

   B. Raw Edge Star:
      - Draw a star shape onto the right side of the front fabric. Lay front and back fabrics wrong sides together and stitch around the star twice, leaving a one-inch gap at the bottom for stuffing. Optional: add trims or Angelina® Fibers to the seams.
      - Trim 1/8 to 1/4 inch outside the stitch line.
3. Stuff your star with polyester filling of choice. Make it fairly firm.
4. When nearly complete, stitch most of the opening closed.
5. Prepare your stitched stick handle (see below). Add stitched ribbons by piercing them with or tying them onto the stick. Apply a thin coat of strong glue to the top of the stick and insert it in the center of the wand. Finish off any remaining closure with hand-stitching.
6. Finish the bottom of the stick with a large bead or add embellishments to your star if desired.

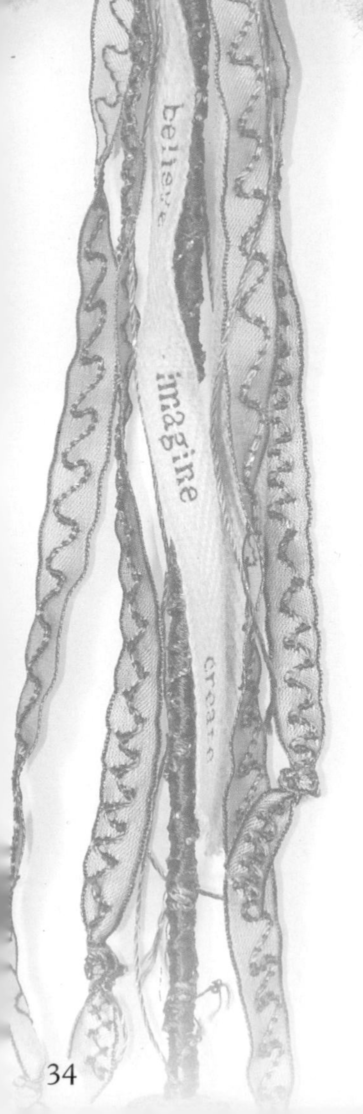

MACHINED CORDS AND STICKS

***You may choose to use safety glasses when stitching on alternative materials!**
Use a decorative yarn, piping cord or long, narrow skewer that easily fits in the channel of a beading foot. Thread the bobbin with Razzle, Dazzle or Sizzle and the top thread with a complementary Rayon color. Set the machine for a wide (7mm), medium length zigzag. Hold both ends of the cord or stick and rapidly move it back and forth through the foot. As thread begins to cover the cord or stick, twirl it around so as to get the heavier thread on all sides of the item. Change threads if desired and stitch until the item no longer passes comfortably under the foot. Apply a dab of glue at the top and bottom to secure threads. The cords and sticks make fabulous dimensional embellishments.

EMERGENCE

Spirit dolls are a unique doll form. They often begin from a very simple pattern but sometimes they demand to become complex, covered in beads and feathers. Every time one is made it can lead to amazing places. Start with one idea and somewhere along the line the doll will take over and makes her own decisions about what she wants to look like and who she wants to be. If you have never made a doll before we encourage you to try a spirit doll. She will open new doors in your mind.

Supplies needed:
Pattern: use ours or draw your own
Base fabric: a fat quarter is enough
Thin quilt batt
Decorative threads: Rayon, Razzle and Dazzle
DecoBob thread that matches your base fabric
Beads, Angelina® Fibers, other embellishments as you like
Face stamp (optional)
Polyfil fiber for stuffing
Stuffing forks or chopsticks/bamboo skewers

Directions:

1. Trace pattern and cut out or make up your own pattern. Draw pattern on the right side of your chosen base fabric. **Note: The pattern outline is the stitching line not a cutting line.** Layer your fabric right side up over a piece of thin quilt batting. Pin baste outside the drawn pattern to keep the layers from shifting.
2. Using a decorative rayon thread and a MYOF technique from your passport pages stitch a design inside the drawn pattern of your doll. When you are finished, trim the excess batting from the back (close to the stitch-line) and press.
3. Add your doll's face details next. Emergence's face is stamped using a stamp from *PostModern Design*. You may choose not to have a face or to hand draw the features you want.
4. Redraw the pattern on the wrong side of your stitched doll fabric. Layer your stitched fabric with the back fabric right sides together, pin baste. Stitch the two layers together using DecoBob and a shortened stitch length. It is helpful to use a shortened stitch length on dolls when you will be trimming seams close to the stitching. Leave an opening on one side of the doll about 1½" long.
5. Trim seam allowance to ⅛", clipping curves and neck joint. Turn doll right side out. Press.
6. Stuff your spirit doll firmly and hand sew opening closed.
7. Your doll is ready for embellishment. Emergence's hair is made up of knotted hanks of Razzle and Dazzle hand-stitched to her head. Three rows of beads dangle from her hands. Angelina® Fibers are fused into a sheet, torn and attached with small stitches to give the impression of cocoon remnants. We suggest that you explore your own dolls unique presentation.

Emergence template: Cut 2 on fold.

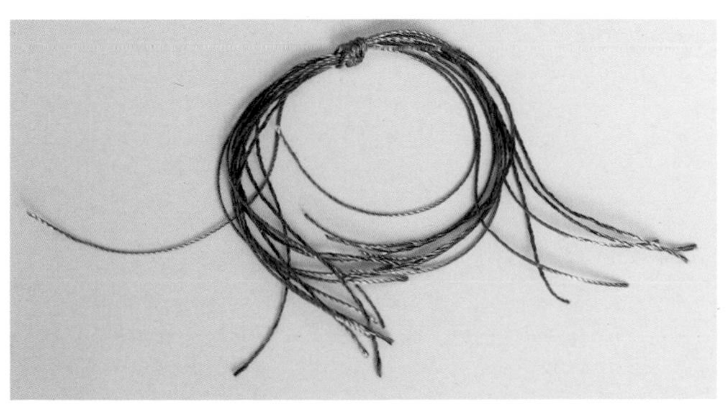

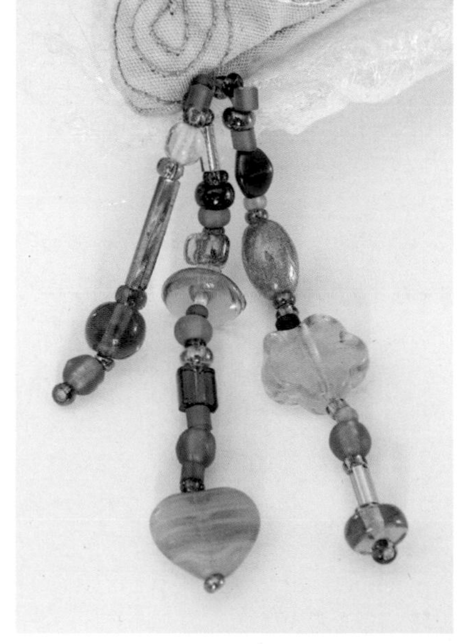

MAKE YOUR OWN STYLE GALLERY

Whether you make a garment yourself or alter something 'off-the-rack,' you can create your own style with WonderFil threads. Accessories can take on a new dimension when you stitch them yourself. Wearing something that you have stitched is one more way to fulfill your love of sewing.

Reversible Vest

Subtle stitching in muted tones stays in keeping with the style of this vest from a Design & Sew pattern (Layers & Layers). On the brown side, Waves were stitched in brown Mirage, while the green side has Box Pivots stitched in variegated green Silco. The stitching was done on the fabric before the pattern was cut out. The result is understated and intriguing.

Tip: Look for tips on using WonderFil thread in your machine embroidery on the Stitchitize web site, www.stitchitize.com. Also, look for free instructions for many embroidery techniques and free embroidery designs.

Textured Scarf

Linda Pidzamecky,
Educator, Janome Sewing Machines Canada

Bold threadwork using Dazzle and DecoBob in the Janome CoverPro 1000CP makes for strong lines that accentuate the design of this original scarf. Linda used a base of fuchsia chiffon topped with raw-edge strips of burgundy organza. The chain stitch is enhanced with the thicker threads.

Thread Artistry Pins

These extraordinary pins will add spice to any ensemble. They are made on a base of felt that is painted with Jacquard Lumiere™ paints and then distressed with a heat gun. Next they are stitched with a variety of free motion stitch patterns using variegated Rayon threads. A second layer of stitching, couching and wrapping is done by hand with Dazzle. Beads are added for a final sparkle. The raw edges of the felt are finished with a fine line of paint. Finally a fabric backing is fused on and a pin back is stitched in place. These are fun and fast to make so you can have one for every outfit!

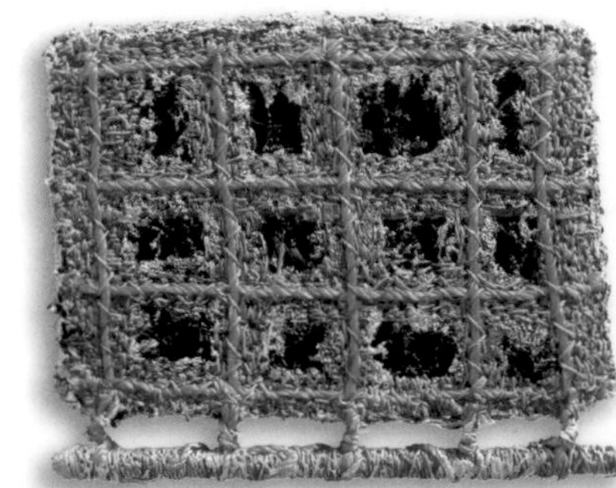

MACHINE EMBROIDERED DETAILS

Denim Jacket

Nancy Storch, WonderFil Specialty Threads

Nancy puts a new spin on machine embroidery with substituting Metallic and D-Twist threads for solid thread colors in this butterfly pattern from Stitchitize. The metallic lends a special touch not usually found in embroidery, while the D-Twist is an easy way to add texture and detail. The botanical details on the front of the jacket are stitched in green Mirage, which gives the effect of several thread changes with one thread.

Nancy recommends a size 16 topstitch needle for embroidering with D-Twist and she uses WonderGuard Thread Wraps whenever embroidering with these specialty threads.

Embroidered Couture

Céline Ross, owner of École de Couture and educator for Janome Canada

Céline uses WonderFil threads in all of her sewing projects. Most of her wardrobe is embroidered in one way or another.

The green suit has been simply stitched in one color of Rayon Embroidery thread for a tone-on-tone effect. Céline likes this embellishment because it does not limit her choices for shoes, blouses or accessories. The design was digitized in multiple colors, but stitched in only one to allow for light and shadow effects.

The yellow tea towel illustrates the use of Accent for heavy thread embroidery. This stitching works especially well with more open designs.

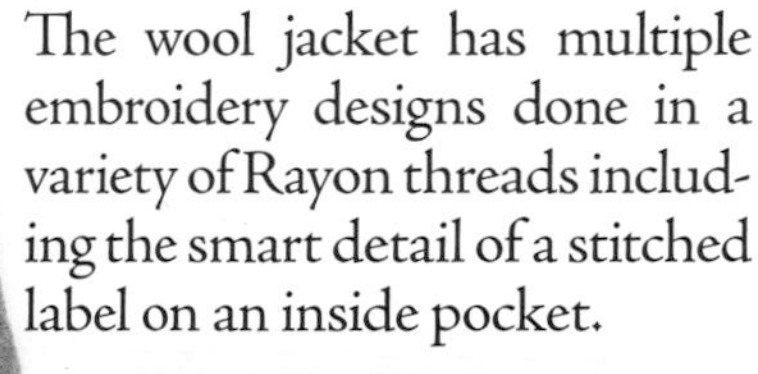

The wool jacket has multiple embroidery designs done in a variety of Rayon threads including the smart detail of a stitched label on an inside pocket.

SASHIKO JOURNAL COVER

Sashiko stitching has traditionally been stitched by hand, but the distinctive look of typically white, heavy thread stitchery, can now be duplicated by machine using Accent thread.
By trying this sampling of patterns in the form of a Journal Cover, you will get a chance to use marking methods and stitch techniques that will give you a sense of sashiko-style methods.

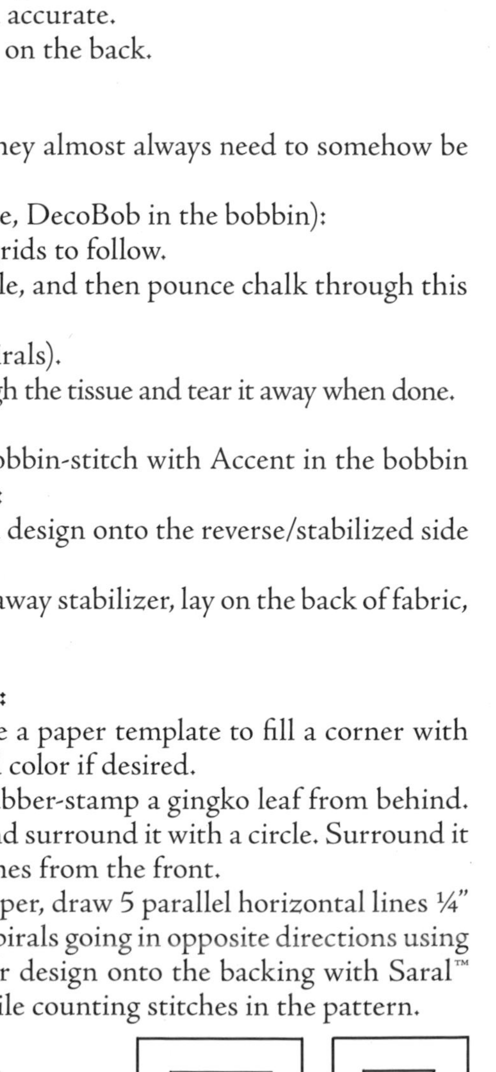

Supplies:
Accent in white and red
DecoBob in black (or to match your fabric color)
Base fabric (black cotton broadcloth)
Fusible, medium weight black stabilizer
Black felt as a liner fabric
Size 16 topstitch needle
Transfer/marking products of choice
Pencils, chalk, transfer paper, tear-away tissue paper

Sashiko basics:
- Lengthen straight stitch length slightly to 2.4 – 2.6
- Avoid traveling over the same stitch line more than once. Plan ahead to minimize these "traveling lines."
- Slightly increase tension for more clean and crisp pivot lines in stitching.
- Try counting the stitches in a repeating pattern. It's easy to do and accurate.
- Stabilize your fabric for crisp stitching and to have a marking base on the back.

Marking Options:
We have found that there are many designs available in sashiko, but they almost always need to somehow be marked on the base fabric.
Marking from the front (stitch from the top with Accent in the needle, DecoBob in the bobbin):
- Use a silver quilting pencil or chalk liner to make small marks or grids to follow.
- Stitch through a paper design template with no thread in the needle, and then pounce chalk through this template to have a print of the design (see chrysanthemum).
- Lay the design over Saral™ Transfer paper and trace it (squared spirals).
- Draw or trace a design onto lightweight, tear away tissue. Stitch through the tissue and tear it away when done.

Marking from the back (bobbin-stitch with Accent in the bobbin and DecoBob in the needle):
- Draw or rubber-stamp a design onto the reverse/stabilized side (Gingko Crest).
- Trace designs onto tear-away stabilizer, lay on the back of fabric, stitch through.

Methods on Journal Cover:
1. Chrysanthemum - make a paper template to fill a corner with the design. Use a second color if desired.
2. Gingko Mon (crest) - rubber-stamp a gingko leaf from behind. Bobbin-stitch the leaf and surround it with a circle. Surround it with a few straight stitches from the front.
3. Squared Spirals - On paper, draw 5 parallel horizontal lines ¼" apart. Draw 2 squared spirals going in opposite directions using the five lines. Trace your design onto the backing with Saral™ paper. Bobbin stitch while counting stitches in the pattern.

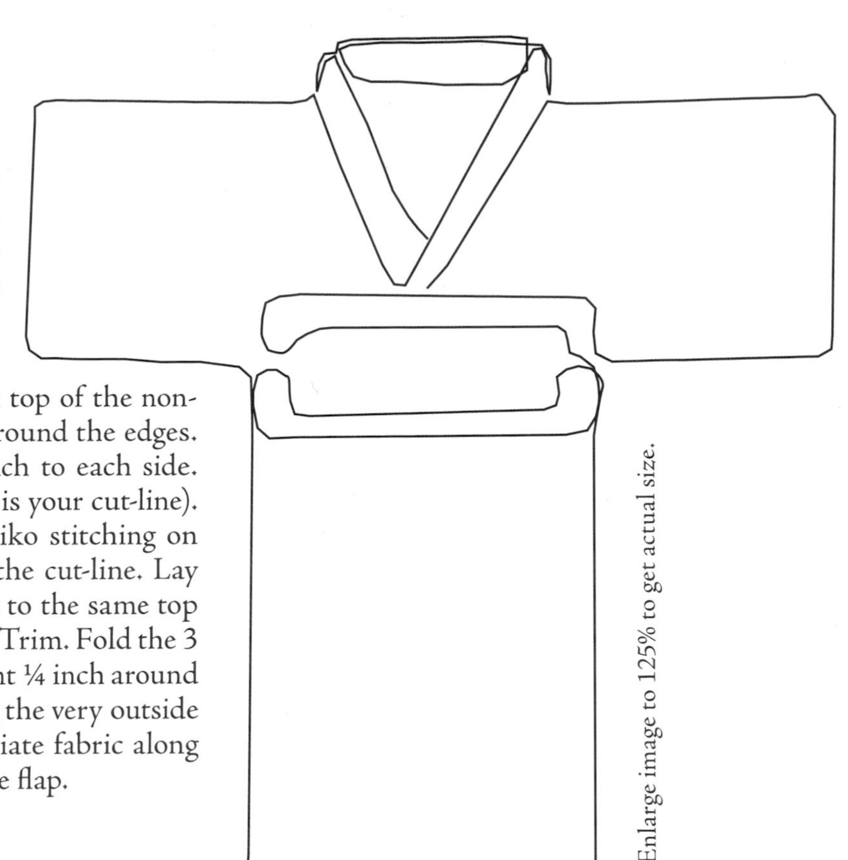

Continuous line kimono: This pattern is designed to show the use of a continuous line in sashiko. Very little of the pattern is retraced. Trace the pattern onto tear-away tissue paper. Pin the tissue in place and machine stitch the pattern.

To make a book cover: Open your journal on top of the non-fusible side of the fusible stabilizer and trace around the edges. Add ¼ inch to the top and bottom and ⅜ inch to each side. Trace a new outline using these additions (this is your cut-line). Fuse stabilizer to black fabric. Complete sashiko stitching on the fabric. Cut out the fused fabric panel on the cut-line. Lay this fabric right side up on black felt. Trim felt to the same top and bottom edge, but add 3 inches to each side. Trim. Fold the 3 inch flaps under each side edge. Top stitch a scant ¼ inch around the entire fabric perimeter. Couch a fiber along the very outside edges if desired. Stitch a torn strip of appropriate fabric along the spine. Tuck the journal covers into each side flap.

STITCHED BOOK ARTS BY CARMI

Carmi Cimicata, www.carmi.ca

Carmi is an accomplished paper artist always looking for new ways to expand her medium. She stitches by hand and machine on many of her paper creations. She feels that this adds another layer of interest and a tactile component to her work. The heavy weights of WonderFil's specialty threads offer new options to the adventurous artist.

P.S. Try creating a passport page stitching on paper.

Altered Book Collage

The pages of this altered book were painted silver and then clocks were rubber-stamped to create the background. Various papers and postage were then glued into place.The pink Accent thread was machine zigzag stitched to create the solid pink lines. The red metallic Dazzle was hand stitched on the right side in a blanket stitch for the edge. On the opposite side the metallic pink Dazzle was used in a blanket stitch with the addition of beads to create that edge. The sentiment was then hand stamped using black StazOn® ink with alphabet stamps. Acrylic paint was used to create the small dots and the small flowers were also stamped using StazOn® ink.

STITCHING ON PAPER

Carmi Cimicata, www.carmi.ca

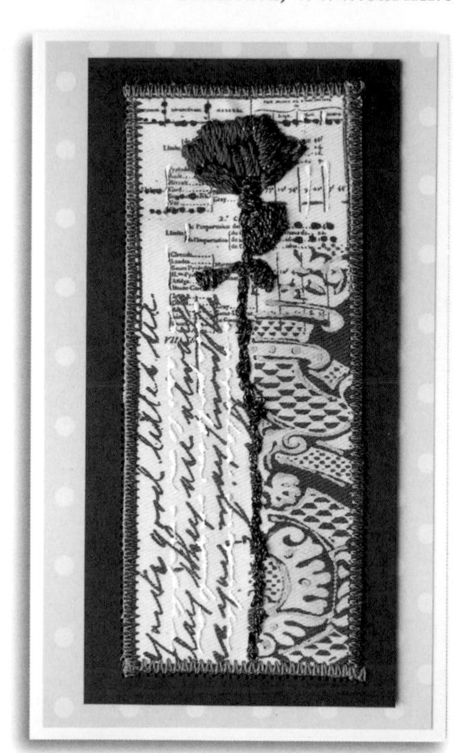

Rose Collage Card

The main image was rubber stamped using black StazOn® ink on white cotton broadcloth. The red rose was hand embroidered using Dazzle. The stem and leaves were also hand embroidered using Sizzle. The image was then machine sewn onto black cardstock using the zigzag stitch and Accent. Ink and paint were used to add color to the background image. The black cardstock, with the image, was then mounted onto the pink and white polka dot paper and then attached to the card. The rubber-stamp is by Christine Adolf and is called *Rose Print*.

Love Folk Art Card

The letters spelling "love" were hand-cut from various fabric remnants. They were hand-stitched onto a piece of handmade paper with Dazzle and Sizzle. The finished paper was then attached to the card and vintage buttons were sewn on the bottom of the card as an embellishment.

Crazy Quilt Card

The small square background pieces of fabric were machine sewn onto a piece of light gray cardstock using the blue Accent and a wide zigzag stitch. The half flower was then cut by hand and also machine stitched into place pink Accent. The "It's your day" fabric sentiment is a pre-purchased embellishment from Memory Makers. The button was the last embellishment to be sewn into place. The entire miniature quilt was then attached to the card front using double-sided tape.

Fabric Strip Card

Strips of various fabrics and pink rickrack were machine sewn onto the front of this ivory card using the pink Accent. The sentiment "Dream with Faith" was printed onto a piece of white cotton and also machine stitched in place. A bottle cap and a vintage image were then used to make the gold-framed female embellishment. This was attached with glue to complete the card.

STITCHED SCRAP BOOK PAPER

Linda Pidzamecky, educator, Janome Sewing Machines Canada

Threadwork enters the field of scrap booking in all sorts of ways. One quick project that can be used many times over is this stitched and copied scrap book paper page. Simply stitch out row upon row of machine patterns. Photocopy the fabric onto sturdy paper and use it in scrap booking. Custom pages can be made in any color or texture to suit a theme.

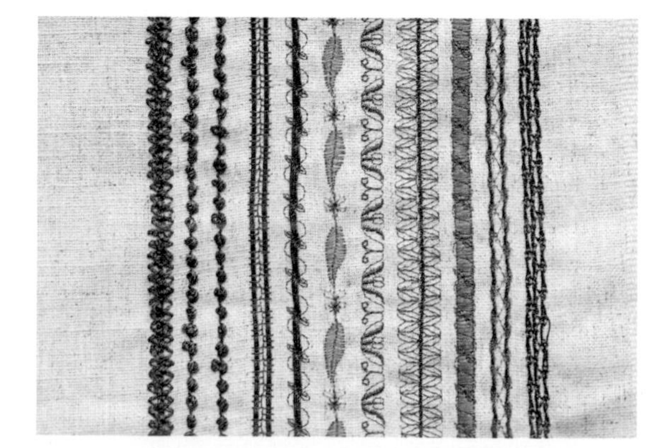

FREE STYLE STITCHED LANDSCAPES

Gordana Brelih

Sunrise

Valley Flowers

Sunset

Gordana is an artist with a natural aptitude for color. She makes her choices seem blissfully easy as she works her fabrics together. She views thread not only as a tool for stitching, but as an extension of her palette. Thread adds bursts of intense color or quiet fields of subdued texture in her work. She encourages readers to try this technique, as it is a small project that uses up scraps and gives you good practice with combining colors.

No work would be complete with some hand stitched thread embellishments. Gordana finds that Accent and Razzle make stitching her multitude of French knots a breeze.

An introduction to freestyle stitching:
Sunrise, Valley Flowers and Sunset are all stitched in the same method:
Threads used include: Rayon Embroidery, D-Twist, Metallic (gold), Accent and Razzle

1. Prepare a fabric sandwich of muslin/batting/flannelette larger than the desired finished size of the piece. In this case frames with a 6" x 6" opening dictated the size.
2. Working from the top of the piece down, fabric is laid in place and stitched. Emphasis is placed on texturing the fabric. A modified ruching technique is used. Oversized fabric is manipulated and pushed into place with a skewer as it is sewn. Rayon Embroidery thread is used for the initial stitching
3. Once the larger, main pieces of fabric have been stitched in place, smaller details are added with fabrics and a variety of machine-stitched threads. Areas that need to be flatter are more heavily stitched.
4. Detailed stitching is added by hand as well as small fabric bits like those that make up the foreground flowers in Sunrise. These can be cut from organza, cotton or silk. They are attached with French knots.
5. The rough shape is trimmed just larger than the mat opening and secured.
6. Don't forget to sign your work!

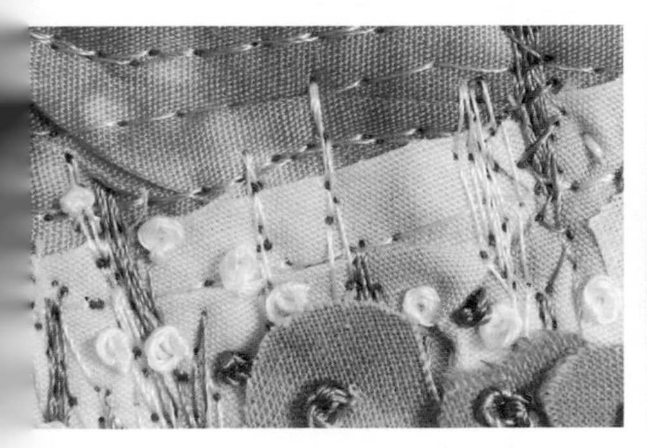

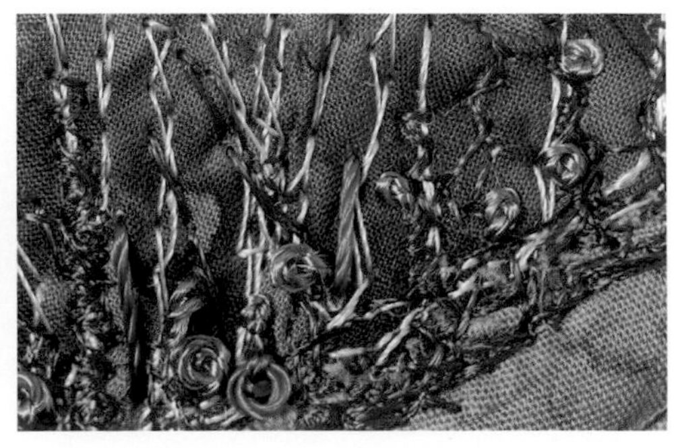

BABY BLESSINGS BOOK

Freestanding accordion books are a wonderful way to commemorate a special event, family member or just record whimsical musings.

The pages are made separately from the backing and can be attached any number of ways including stitches, glue, grommets or ribbons. This book consists of 4 pages mounted to a back that is the actual foldable piece, which stands upright. The back is fabric-covered Fast2Fuse™ stabilizer. Timtex™ can also be used. The backing fabric is fused with the edges turned under for a clean finish. The outside edges of the backing are finished with a zigzag stitch that is then covered with a trim.

Each page is made individually over a stabilizer base (light to mid-weight Pellon™ or Vilene™) and then mounted onto the backing with craft glue. There are many things you can include in your book, from photos to keepsakes, there are no rules.

1. The cover for the Baby Blessings Book gets lots of texture and movement from the use of Accent thread in seed and running stitches. A decorative machine stitch in rayon frames the photo, which is dotted with French knots of Silco thread. "Blessings" is machine embroidered.
2. The "Cherish" page features hand-stitched accents in the toile pattern using Rayon thread. The print is surrounded by a beaded blanket stitch done in Silco. More seed stitching is on the gingham surrounding "Cherish."
3. The "Hope" page features four layers of fabric simply straight stitched atop one another with Silco. A coordinating ribbon is hand-stitched as well as flower petals with pearl accents.
4. The pocket page lets vintage linen, lace and a button be the stars. Machine and hand stitching embellish the tags that further the theme.

CONFETTI HEARTS

Fabric confetti: those little bits of past projects that get scattered around your cutting table like the remnants of a wild sewing party! Why not put them to good use in this project that can be a decorative ornament or a functional pincushion. These hearts are made of layers of stabilizer, fabrics bits and stitches. Lots of stitches! The wings are optional and are made using the same techniques as with the thread grids.

P.S. You might try this technique as a Passport Page or you can use it to make fabric for other small projects like a book cover or cosmetic bag.

1. Start with a piece of fusible stabilizer larger than the finished heart size. Lay it fusible side up on the ironing board.
2. Scatter bits of assorted fabrics to cover the stabilizer. Lay a pressing sheet over this collage and press to secure the bits. You may choose to work on one fabric only. In this case, fuse stabilizer to that one fabric.
3. Optional: add a layer of tulle or organza over the top of the collage.
4. Gather an assortment of threads and start stitching! You may wish to first mark or stitch random lines to divide the surface into distinct areas. Either way, choose a stitch and a thread and go. Stitch rows of the same pattern close together. Repeat until an area is filled. Shift the fabric, change the thread and the stitch, and repeat. Cover the fabric in stitching. Open, airy stitches let the fabric confetti show through, while satin stitches will dominate the finished heart.
5. If desired, stitch wings on water-soluble stabilizer as with the thread grids. Rinse away the stabilizer and dry the wings.
6. Pin two layers of confetti fabric wrong sides together. Mark a heart shape and cut along the line.
7. Tuck the edges of the wings just inside the heart and a ribbon or thread for hanging. Stitch the hearts together using Accent thread and a narrow zigzag stitch, leaving a gap for stuffing. Stitch around the heart again with a slightly wider zigzag.
8. Fill the heart (not too firmly) with polyester stuffing and hand or machine stitch the heart closed.
9. If the heart will be a pincushion, you may want to tack a small piece of rubberized shelf lining to the back to keep it from slipping off the table. Add beads or embellish as desired.

Color, texture, and visual excitement: these three factors play a major role in the fabric dolls that Heike creates. She is motivated to change plain fabrics into something that you just have to touch it to see how it feels. She loves to make pieces that look as if they have grown on the doll instead of being stitched on. The more layers, the better! When it comes to stitching with WonderFil, with so many different colours and thread weights to chose from, Heike will never run out of ideas.

AZULLA

Heike Blohm, blohm-gagne@rogers.com

Lace Flowers

- Cut a flower shape from ordinary lace and back it with a slightly larger piece of organza.
- Layer lace and organza between two larger pieces of heavy weight water-soluble stabilizer.
- Choose your Rayon Embroidery thread and machine stitch pattern. It is important to have the same thread in the bobbin in case it shows through.
- Start stitching near the center of the flower to the outer edge. If you sew off of the lace, it lends a more organic look to the finished piece.
- Continue with each petal. Switch patterns and threads for a more textured look.
- Note: Variegated threads done in a satin stitch will have an added "Wow!" factor. Try a contrast in color for extra punch.
- When you have done enough stitching, rinse the piece in warm water until the stabilizer has completely dissolved. Lay flat to dry. The finished flower may be a bit stiff after drying, which is normal.
- Do not trim off thread bits! They add to the charm of the piece.
- Sew beads in the middle of the flower. Try a button, or French knots done with Razzle thread.
- Take a length of Dazzle thread in a contrasting color and do some hand stitching on the petals; i.e. a daisy stitch.
- Hand-sew the finished piece in place with a few well-placed stitches.
- Variation of the Lace Flower: Cut pieces of lightweight silk, organza or fine netting into petal shapes. Arrange the pieces in between layers of water-soluble stabilizer to form flower shapes. Follow the instructions for the lace flowers to finish the pieces.

Skirt, Bodice & Wings

- Using different colors of lightweight silks, organzas, chiffons and fine netting, cut out long shapes in various sizes. Heike uses pointed ovals or petal shapes for this.
- Arrange the pieces, with at least 3 layers in most spots, on a large piece of fine netting. When you are happy with the look of the layers, place another large piece of fine netting over top and pin the various layers together. Pieces will shift but don't worry about it.
- Pick your stitch and thread types. For the Rayon and Mirage, use the same thread in the bobbin as it will show through. Try to catch as many layers as possible with the first bit of stitching.
- Switch thread types, colors and stitch patterns as often as you wish until you feel the piece is finished. If you don't trim the thread ends off, you have a more magical look.
- Hand beading and embroidery using the Razzle, Dazzle or Mirage threads help create more texture.
- To keep the wings stiffer, zigzag stitch Mirage thread over fine wire in a spiral shape on the wings.
- The skirt follows the same technique outlined above but used much larger pieces of organza with the top layer bunched up a bit for more dimension.

Ribbon Crown

- Cut leafy organza shapes in different colors and sizes.
- Lay a few lengths of organza ribbons in 2 different colours and widths along water-soluble stabilizer that is as long as the ribbon and three times as wide.
- Arrange the "leaves" on the ribbons, being sure to overlap them a bit.
- Fold the stabilizer over top of the ribbons and "leaves". Pin in place through all the layers.
- Using a rayon thread in the bobbin as well. Stitch a few lines of straight stitch from one end of the ribbon sandwich to the other to secure them. The tops of the leaves will remain free.
- Switch to variegated Rayon or Mirage threads. Choose a stitch pattern and sew across the width of the "sandwich" a few times.
- When finished, rinse the piece in warm water till the stabilizer is gone. Leave thread ends hanging. When the piece is dry, roll it into the desired size cylinder shape and sew all the layers together by hand along the bottom of the cylinder.
- Add some French knots, using the Dazzle thread, and beads along the bottom edge for more texture. Now all you need are some ribbons trailing from the back of the crown and you are all set. Add a few lengths of metallic thread mixed with the ribbons for extra sparkle.

STITCHED STORIES IN FABRIC BOOKS

In all that we create, we tell our story. Rich with personal nuance, our color choices, shapes and subjects reveal our thoughts and emotions. Sometimes the threads sing with happiness and sometimes they say what we cannot otherwise express. Use your thread to tell your story. Consider possible themes in fiction or nonfiction. Maybe you want to express a poem or celebrate a life event. The possibilities are boundless!

These are some suggestions to get you started in stitching fabric books:

- Fabric books can be put together in the same fashion as your passport. Determine a page size and make a template for keeping page size and buttonhole or grommet placement consistent.
- Assess your technique possibilities. Look at your passport. What do you want to try?
- You will need to plan a cover page and a few 'signatures.' Signatures are the groupings of pages that form a page unit. In this case a signature is 2 pages, front and back, bound together around the outside edges. These are placed sequentially on the binder rings, behind the cover.
- It sometimes helps to make a paper layout of your book to get a clear idea of how the pages will flow together.
- Stitch each page separately before binding them together. Remember to consider all of your different threads when stitching. Use them to add bursts of color and texture. Add text. Free-motion stitch a figure or appliqué. Use your different edge finish techniques around the bound edges of the pages. You have learned a wide variety of techniques in your journey. A fabric book is a perfect opportunity to express your unique ideas in stitching.

Where Will You Journey To?

These final pages bring us back home with suitcases overflowing with souvenir projects and a passport filled with stitches. Hopefully, you have enjoyed the journey and have many tales of sewing adventures to share with your stitching friends. We also hope this journey has sparked a bit of wanderlust in your soul and ignited the fearless traveler in your heart.

We encourage you to continue to explore both familiar and uncharted territory with your needle and threads. Ask yourself "what if?" And don't forget to send us a postcard.

Deb & Liz

ONE LAST PROJECT!

There's a little space left on the last page? Well, then there is room for one more project!

Bohemian: A person with artistic or literary interests who disregards conventional standards of behavior.

The Boho Bag
Most of us carry purses. They come in all shapes and sizes to suit our personalities. The next time you need a purse, why not make your own? Choose a favorite pattern or just "wing it." Cover it in threadwork.
This bag features thread in three ways:

- Programmed machine embroidery from the Janome MC 11000.
- A thread appliqué done as a 'dangle' by applying it to a felt backing
- Free-stitched squares:
  These squares consist of fusible stabilizer covered with fabric and randomly stitched threads. In this case, 3 base fabrics were used: orange organza, pink tulle and melon silk. The larger squares were stitched and then all were cut into 1½" squares. These smaller squares were then fused in a grid on the purse fabric and stitched in place. Machined cords were couched around the grid.

Work with your favorite threads, in your favorite colors, on your favorite fabric. Let your style shine and let the world know that you love to stitch!

Traveling helps you grow because it forces you to take risks. The subject matter and atmosphere are different.
~ Marilyn Simandle

Resources

Stitch Journeys Selected Reading List:

We have tried to give you an introduction to many thread techniques made all the more exciting with WonderFil Specialty Threads. The authors cited below are all experts in the field with their own unique approaches to threadwork, embroidery and creative stitchery. We highly recommend and admire their work.

All about Machine Arts: Decorative Techniques from A to Z, C&T Publishing
Anything written by Jan Beany and Jean Littlejohn
Color and Composition for the Creative Quilter, Katie Pasquini Masopust & Brett Barker
Color Fusion, Laura Heine
Coloring with Thread, Ann Fahl
Contemporary Quilts: Design, Surface and Stitch, Sandra Meech
Embroidered Boxes, or Three Dimensional Embroidery, Janet Edmonds
Free Expression: The Art and Confessions of a Contemporary Quilter, Robbi Joy Eklow
Machine Embroidery or any other book by Valerie Campbell-Harding
Paper, Metal & Stitch, Maggie Grey & Jane Wild
Quilted Memories, Lesley Riley
Thread Magic: The Enchanted World of Ellen Anne Eddy, Ellen Anne Eddy
Threadplay, Libby Lehman

Rubber-stamps: (pg #, name, company)

24, Pear, www.stampersanonymous.com
31, The Caligraphy Robe, Stampington & Co
31, Art washes, Inkadinkado
35, Worldly doll face, Postmodern Design
38, Gingko Leaf, www.purrfection.com

Thread Catchers custom made by
Michele Bremner
Email: skyelark@sympatico.ca

On-Line Resources:

www.wonderfil.net (see all of the threads and suppliers)
www.stitchitize.com (sells the full WonderFil line)
www.joggles.com (textile art & mixed media supplies)
www.aneedlepullingthread.com (A Needle Pulling Thread, fabulous Canadian magazine)
www.quiltingartsllc.com (Quilting Arts, fabulous American magazine)
www.jacquardproducts.com (luscious Lumiere paints)
www.kuninfelt.com (felt to distress, stitch & paint)
www.painterskeys.com (Robert Genn's art/life newsletter)

Debbie & Liz

Once upon a time two different women set out from two different houses with three different kids. They walked on different sides of the street to and from the park. They waved to one another, and thus began a friendship of a lifetime. Liz taught Debbie to sew and Debbie taught Liz to play. Together they have developed their own unique approach to stitching and formed Goddess Within Designs. Despite the miles between them, this duo creates, teaches and designs as a partnership. They use fabrics, fibers and mixed media to draw forth and express the weathered, wise and unique artistic visions that they believe are within all women. They feel that each woman needs only to seek, try and ask "what if?" to undertake her stitch journey. Every woman has a personal mythology to be told: in her voice, with her hands, from her soul. Debbie and Liz would be honored to walk a while with others on this journey.

Debbie is based in Newmarket, Ontario, while Liz is in Monument, Colorado. Each has developed her own style and teaching repertoire. Debbie's work has been in A Needle Pulling Thread and Cloth, Paper, Scissors. She is an educator with Janome Canada. Liz shows her work locally and currently has a quilt traveling with The Alzheimer's Art Quilt Initiative (www.AlzQuilts.com), a program to raise awareness and fund research for Alzheimer's disease.
Their work can be seen at www.goddesswithindesigns.com. Drop by and share where you have traveled with your passport!